Port Camargue (France)

Photo © 2021 Gilles Bonifay

Destiny

From a lived experience to a theory

GILLES BONIFAY

© 2021 BONIFAY, GILLES
Édition:BoD – Books on Demand, 12/14 rond-point des ChampsÉlysées, 75008 Paris
Impression : BoD - Books on Demand, Norderstedt, Allemagne
ISBN : 9782322191123
Dépôt légal : Février 2021

Preface

Life is not always a peaceful experience. Each one of us trusts the five conventional senses to evolve physically and psychically in this particular time that accompanies us from birth to death. Since the 18th century, common human thought has emphasized reason and excluded everything that escapes the ambient rationalism. Thus, man is considered as an entity that is divided between materiality and spirituality. Words are too often imprecise and cannot cover the subtlety of the different states of the human being. The authentic meanings of materiality and spirituality are understood in different ways according to beliefs, traditions, and philosophies. It is not always easy to recognize oneself in certain approaches. How can we favour one or the other of these orientations when we seem to be fundamentally identical and only personal convictions allow us to choose one or the other proposal of wisdom. We lack lived experiences to deepen our existence.

Destiny is a pretext for the reader to make an inner journey in all sincerity. Through an experience, which he himself has lived, the author invites us to journey towards wider horizons, in a generous quest. The place of man is revisited. Both in the universe but also at the confluence of the visible and the invisible. A meeting place between the animate and the inanimate, the accessible and the inaccessible, this space is shared by many and ignored by the greatest number. Scientific dogmatism rejects what cannot be factually verified by refuting the fundamental aporism of the human being in its complexity and multiplicity.

The experts went through moments of spontaneous and intense unveiling that opened up new dimensions. Between reverie, imagination and intuition, they are confronted with concepts which, to a greater or lesser extent, still resemble the traces left by prehistoric man on cave walls and shamanic activities, which can still be observed in areas preserved from the harmful influences of urban civilisation. These observations invite us to reconsider the idea of a primordial tradition based on the integration of humans into a sphere of consciousness common to all the energy forms of the universe.

Science describes and comments on how things work, but is unable to give them true and, for many, mysterious meaning. By seeking to dichotomize the formal states of man, science seeks to be the guardian of superficial orthodox knowledge. The opposition between traditional and modern sciences sterilizes the field of knowledge. It is up to each of us to explore the different components of the forces, energies and forms that surround us. Keeping spontaneity and the thirst for knowledge in all circumstances is an excellent practice to allow oneself to be penetrated by all realities with great serenity and clear-sightedness. Each reality refers us to our own study and finitude.

The Western Judeo-Christian vision suggests to man that he is the only representative of intelligent life, and that life is bounded by the will of a higher power, which reigns here and there. Death and the eschatological future of the individual are ontological concerns that have been questioning Homo sapiens for more than 100,000 years. But in doing so, these two obsessions question us about phenomena and existences other than those described by academic human norms. In this book, the questions asked are legitimate and address what more we have within us, buried in the depths of our esoteric knowledge.

Jean-Michel Ballester
Microbiologist

Today, I am not facing a blank sheet of paper, I am in possession of my 14 pages written in the 90s about my stay in Niort (Deux-Sèvres, France) as part of my intervention as an Information Systems Consultant for MACIF. Initially, this book was to be limited to telling the story of this rather disturbing period; then, as the years went by, I managed to mature, to build my theory and finally I wanted to share it.

Thus, after 25 years of reflection, I am launching myself to finalize this project. I take notes, extracts from newspaper articles, drafts, without giving any bibliographical references because at the beginning I did not read on this subject: I did not want to be influenced.

Originally, the question of belief arises: I am a non-practising believer. If I had to introduce myself, I would say the following: "*I am Catholic for being part of its community, Buddhist for its philosophy of life, Jewish for its solidarity and its recognition of the great prophets, Muslim for its rigour and its positioning of God*". This must seem strange to the reader. Yet religions have gone beyond their role of adapting concepts to a particular way of life according to a specific climate or geography. Man has fewer and fewer constraints linked to his place of residence, less and less dependence on the society of which he is a part of, fewer specific ties at a social level. The means of communication, transport and the media are gradually breaking down disinformation or isolation to offer a global, worldwide and objective approach to get closer to our truth. Of course, we are only at the beginning, especially in terms of objectivity ... but the first advances in this field allow us to see ourselves and our environment differently.

The greatest difficulty is to separate ourselves from the dogmas we are taught, our education, our pre-written logic and our purpose, imposed in a society where life is a frenetic race, and success is measured above all by our financial means. My experience has forced me to question everything and to find coherence based on fundamentals to become aware of my reality.

"the noblest task of the individual is to become self-aware"
Carl Gustav Jung, Swiss psychiatric doctor

My approach is based on my experience, my background, my knowledge. I try to share my vision rigorously.
It is divided into three parts:

1. The first part describes my experience during two important events in my life: the first was climbing Mount Kilimanjaro in Tanzania in 1987 when I had no high mountain skills and the second is about a period of more than a year in 1992 during which I lived in a haunted house in the town of Niort when I was not prepared for this experience.

2. The second part presents concepts on which my experience has allowed me to open my mind to fundamental questions such as: what is life? or death? or consciousness? and finally God? I will use my own concepts to follow up on my observations about ghosts, spirits, our interactions.

3. The third part brings a development to my approach on destiny, or rather on our destiny because we are all intimately linked.

Everything should converge towards one and only one result: our reality.

This book hopes to contribute to a new way of thinking that speaks openly about subjects usually reserved for a handful of people. I therefore approach these important themes with as much humility as originality I believe. May this reflection bring its piece to the understanding of this Universe comparable to the edifice of a linked and harmonized whole in which every living being contributes amply to the construction, the evolution, the finality.

« We're just an advanced race of apes on a small planet of a medium star. But we can understand the Universe. That makes us something incredibly special. »
Stephen Hawking, British astrophysicist

I understand this book is ambitious, that it cannot be an unanimous work. However, should we give up nevertheless? That is not my way of looking at life. I even decided to go further and to add elements on my conception of earthly life. And this is how I came to talk about Destiny.

This book addresses people looking for a reflection on the meaning of our existence, believers who wish to approach the subject in a different way, who appreciate a global approach on a global subject.

First part

The experiences on which my evidence is based

« It's not enough to think our destiny, we have to feel it…»

Miguel de Unamuno
« Tragic sense of life» 1913

We are all masters of our own destiny …

Friday, August 14, 1987. Kilimanjaro, Tanzania. My first certainties.

I remember my personal reflections during the final ascent of Mount Kilimanjaro where, exhausted by the lack of oxygen and the fatigue of the previous days, I wondered
why was I even here! and above all, why take such risks!

Is there a before and after?
Was my life going to be better when I got back?
How was this project important to me?
What was my reason for being in Tanzania, far from home and where, above all, any problem could have dramatic consequences?

The 4,000 meters of altitude are exceeded...
Each additional step requires a real effort...
And yet I want to take that extra step!
It is in these situations that we see the strength of the mind and the submission of the body.

At 4,700 meters, a group of Frenchmen is at the entrance to the last refuge. Night falls on the mountain and after a few exchanges with my compatriots, one of them lights a cigarette, takes two puffs and falls to the ground. Luckily, at the same time, a German doctor arrives at the refuge: he immediately starts a cardiac massage. The young man's heart quickly starts to beat again. The doctor orders him to go back down immediately, and he and his friends do the same. His ascent is over!

After a few attempts to rest, it is time to leave: four o'clock in the morning. I resume the ascent towards Gillman's point at 5683 meters. Once again, my questions arise: what is the link between mind and body? My mind has decided this ascent, but is my body in agreement with this objective? I can find motivations for my mind, but what are those for my body?

I am exhausted, each new step is a physical challenge. Then I remember the quote from the American writer William Arthur Ward:
« *"It's impossible," said pride.*
"It's risky," said experience.
"It's pointless," said reason.
"Give it a try." whispered the heart ».

And this time the heart wins. The rim of the crater appears with the sunrise despite the clouds hanging over the summit. As soon as it is reached, a few photos to immortalize the moment, a few hugs with those of the group and the people present who are experiencing the same event and then it is the descent back down to avoid complications related to the altitude of the 5685 meters of Gillman's point.

This experience allowed me to get to know myself better, not without reason. My body surpassed itself in suffering by the will of my spirit to give my life a meaning.

A new image comes to mind: that of the rider with his horse, a tournament, jumps, risks taken in solidarity, in communion I would say. What interest does the horse have in this? To please the horseman? To live in symbiosis or even in osmosis with its rider whom it sees on a daily basis?
To me, this link between the rider and his horse seems to be identical to the link between body and spirit: only the spirit can

define the path to take in order to reach his earthly goal. But he needs his body to do so. The body is a mean of expressing oneself while considering the limits of anatomy and physiology.

I also imagined life on earth as a treadmill: I decide to go on it, I try not to fall on the sides, knowing that I will fall one day ... I don't know when. But that day will come, it is THE certainty. We can all bless every new day, but what is the point? A few days more or less, what's the point if we don't have goals? Do I have a purpose? What do I bring? To whom? For we are all born to be useful. Human usefulness is not only reserved to a chosen few. But to make our usefulness manifest itself, each individual must first get to know himself.

« *By letting our own light shine,*
we unconsciously give others the power to do the same ».
Marianne Williamson, A Return to Love[1]

By allowing me to know my abilities, to know the strengths of my mind, this ascension taught me who I am. The direction to take gradually became obvious: I remain master of my destiny like a driver in his vehicle, deciding on his route which roads to take, the speed to adopt, whether or not to stop on the roadside... Only the starting and finishing points are defined in advance. The route chosen is generally predictable: the most obvious, but not guaranteed. So, a driver who has to travel from Marseille to Paris has a good chance of taking the shortest and safest route. He will take the motorway. This is not a certainty but a high probability. He will arrive at his destination. It is not a certainty but a high probability. The journey will take about seven hours. It is not a certainty but a high probability. The driver may decide otherwise during the journey, decide to take the national highway

---

[1] Excerpt from the book published in 1992. Taken up by Nelson Mandela during his presidential inauguration speech in 1994.

temporarily or permanently, stop for a longer or shorter time, drive faster or slower, or stop his life altogether.

He remains in control of his destiny.

From June '91 to February '93. Niort. Deux-Sèvres, France. My first convictions.

Ghost stories never interested me until I was confronted with one...

Is it mere coincidence or the consequences of a pre-established destiny?

In any case, this year-long experience has become a defining moment in my life. And this book is the proof: it was written more than twenty years later, twenty years of reflections and questioning that led to a theory. The term is a bit strong, you might say? However, I am going to propose a set of ideas, abstract concepts applied to a specific field. I am going to build a system of hypotheses with rules that seem logical to me... I leave that judgment to you alone!

Over the past twenty years, I have had the opportunity to share my experience with many people interested in the subject, whether or not sceptical. With hindsight, I am now convinced that I have radically reoriented my life since that experience, because, in the end, the question of destiny is the main question to ask oneself. This period was the trigger for my questioning. However, the answers remain very personal while waiting for the firm and definitive results of science. But how long will we have to wait? How many generations?

This true story serves as a springboard for the other two parts of the book, which are based on much more general reflections.

Thursday, June 22, 1991. Cergy, Val d'Oise, France. On the road to my destiny.

Back then, my postgraduate studies were coming to an end. One or two more seminars integrated into the programme of this master's degree from the prestigious "Ecole Supérieure des Sciences Economiques et Commerciales (ESSEC)" and then it will be the internship. It will take place in the IT department of the Thomson Video Equipment Company, a subsidiary of the Thomson CSF group in high definition television. That is how I spent a year living in Cergy, one of the new towns created from scratch to ease traffic in Paris. Despite my many requests to the university halls of residence, I could not find a place there. I decided to rent a small studio of 18 square meters near the RER stop "Cergy prefecture". It seemed that I was lucky to find this accommodation ... it's quite hard to digest for a provincial to be "lucky" enough to find a studio worth the rent of a three-room apartment in the 5 avenues district in Marseille, 5th.

After that period, I looked for a job. Wanting to come back to the South of France, my job search in this region did not really satisfy my interests. Only analyst-programmer positions were offered to me, whereas in Paris, I was offered IT manager positions. What to choose? Career or quality of life? This is a subject that could be the subject of several books ... but for me, it will be the quality of life, trying to avoid routine or uninteresting work. A great challenge in a country where, at the time, IT was still extremely centralized, where two thirds of computer scientists worked in the Paris region!

One day, a job offer on the weekly magazine "zéro un informatique" calls out to me. It is an IT engineering service and consulting company offering positions based in Paris, Niort and Marseille. I decided to apply.

A few days later, a letter offers me an interview. And, after following the classic selection procedure, my two future managers, founders of the Company, offer me a position as a consulting engineer based in Marseille! The hiring date is set for November 1, 1989, after my dissertation has been defended and my postgraduate diploma validated. The founders of this company are graduates of the "Grandes Ecoles". They got to know each other while working for the TOTAL Company. The environment seems interesting to me. I accept their offer.

My First interventions

My first intervention will be in Boulogne in the Paris region at a major French car manufacturer: Renault. The subject is interesting: I must improve the user-friendliness and security of a data query product "Query Management Facility" marketed by IBM. I am on the road and returning to Marseille for the weekend. For convenience reasons, I have kept my studio, which is paid for by my employer. Like most Parisians, I have more than an hour's travel time on the outward journey and as much on the return journey. Let's go for the metro/work/sleep rhythm!

Then I had the opportunity to visit new clients around the city of Nice. Some consulting missions started with training courses in information systems design. This was followed by audits, which were to lead to longer assignments, which would allow me to "hook the client". In light of this experience, a mission in Niort was proposed to me to reinforce the existing team of consultants. Niort is a town in the centre-west of France, capital of the "Deux-Sèvres" department. A team of four people was working on the biggest IT project in France at the moment: the overhaul of the information system of the "Mutuelle Assurance des Commerçants et Industriels de France (M.A.C.I.F.)". This subject was of great interest to me. I accepted immediately and left for Niort in the summer of 1990.

In fact, two other consultants from the Paris region had also been asked to complete the team: Xavier F. and Robin P. Both computer engineers, fresh out of school.

At the end of the first fortnight, the head of Niort subsidiary, Jean D., quickly offered to rent a house to accommodate the three of us. We would thus make substantial savings in costs and it would make life more pleasant for us as part of this mobility.

Fabienne the secretary oversaw making a first selection with simple criteria such as the number of rooms (three minimum), proximity to the workplace and a budget not to be exceeded.

Initial research showed that the choice would be limited: it would be difficult to find a house with three bedrooms, furnished if possible. The proximity of the town of Niort was an important parameter for Jean but the town centre was forbidden to us for a question of cost. After having visited all the estate agencies in the region, Fabienne obtained about ten addresses, visited the premises and then submitted her selection to Jean. When our opinion was sought, the list was reduced to three addresses. Appointments were made for us to visit them.

The first visit took place about 15 minutes from the city. From the beginning, Jean made us understand that this choice was not ideal. A large garden of about one hectare, mainly at the back of the house. A rather banal interior: I remember rather small rooms, an exceptionally large garage, and horrible tapestries, "baba cool" type in very bright colours. There was no character and no love at first sight.

The second visit took us to Niort to see a construction that had just been completed. The small plot of land looked more like a building site than a garden: no planting and above all a lot of mud! The interior space, on one level only, was quite small. The two Parisians quickly vetoed this possible selection. They later confessed to me that it was mainly because of the mud that could have dirtied their beautiful recently bought consultant suits!

The third visit allowed us to go to the city near outskirts, in the direction of the village of Parthenais. Its proximity to the highway made this place noisy. On the other hand, there was space outside as well as inside: this old farm was fitted out with a large inner courtyard allowing us to park our cars. It was surrounded by annexes such as an old pigsty and, adjoining the house, an old stable.

This house was at a dead end. It ended a series of houses overlooking the expressway that allowed vehicles to avoid the downtown area. The cul-de-sac became a narrow alley at the same level as the house, easily noticeable by its great height. A white gate allowed access to an inner courtyard bounded by a long shed on the right that could be used as a garage for our three cars. Opposite, a sparse hedge adorned at its right end by a large and beautiful acacia tree. This tree, about fifteen meters high, reminded me of its African cousins admired in Tanzania four years earlier. On the left, perpendicular to the building, four medium-sized but very bushy mulberry trees were home to many birds, mainly blackbirds. This courtyard thereby delimited represents more than two hundred square metres, half covered with burgundy gravel and grass on the hedge side. An iron door painted white allowed access to the kitchen. To the left of the kitchen was an entrance to two stables and to the right was the entrance to the house itself. The first room, which was rarely used, contained a fireplace closed with an iron plate and was followed by the stairwell and the entrance to the living room. This staircase led to two bedrooms and a bathroom on the first floor, then to two bedrooms and a small storage room on the second and top floor.

That old farmhouse was gloomy and dark.

I remember I was the first to accept it for a purely practical reason: it seemed to me more suitable for a life in a community, especially with its two toilets, unlike the other dwellings. But also, for its proximity to the city centre and the workplace. The two Parisians hesitated at first, but then accepted. Jean organized himself so that, starting at the beginning of September 1990, we could settle there by ordering and delivering very quickly cheap furniture from a French furniture and decoration retailer well known at that time: FLY. The choices were directed by Marie, Jean's wife, and executed by Fabienne.

Water and electricity were switched on, the telephone installed. The house, however, seemed to have been uninhabited for some time: spiders had taken over in all the living rooms as well as dust in the outbuildings and weeds in the garden.

It was time to choose a room. I did not have a preference for neither of the rooms. Indeed, on the first floor there were two bedrooms, one large but close to the bathroom and WC, the other small. Being on the first floor was not a decisive advantage: when one was doing sit-down work all day long, climbing two floors up a spiral staircase seemed like an interesting exercise to keep in shape. On the second floor there was the largest room in the house next to a small bedroom.

As soon as we arrived, Robin rushed to one of the two rooms on the first floor. Xavier seemingly had no more opinion than I did. After much politeness, we agreed that Xavier would take the small room on the first floor. This left the whole second floor for me alone. I moved my things into the large room.

Monday, September 2, 1991. Niort, Deux-Sèvres, France. My first contacts.

The purpose of my intervention at MACIF was to coordinate and organize the unit tests of the major information system redesign project. I liked this mission and I worked without counting the hours. So, I sometimes left work at around seven or eight in the evening. After a quick meal, I wanted only one thing: to sleep! All the more so as for that first night in the house, my arrival was late: around eleven o'clock at night. So, I settled down in this large bed under a duvet representing a palm tree under a blazing sun. It was with this last image in mind that I turned off the little bedside lamp. There was no sign of the strange night I was about to spend...
I was beginning to fall asleep when I felt a presence in the room. Assuming that a colleague was playing a joke to scare me or was curious about my installation, I did not feel any sense of insecurity. I simply turned on my bedside lamp and at that moment I realized that I was alone. This surprise gradually turned into confusion because the light did not suppress the feeling: there was still someone in front of me! Halfway between the closed bedroom door and the bed looking at me without moving.

My first reaction was to sit in my bed, taking the time to look into every corner of the room to discover any kind of details that could explain this situation. Then came doubt and questioning about what I was feeling. My thoughts were no longer clear in my head. What could be easier in this situation than to think that imagination is playing tricks on us!

Sleep took over, I decided to turn off the light and forget the feeling. As soon as the light went out, the presence became more pronounced and began to approach the bed. Convinced that I was delirious, I quickly pulled the duvet up to my nose. This shield should have been enough to fight my own imagination, but in vain! A foot or so separated us now. What could I do? I turned the lamp back on to confirm once again that I was alone in the room. And yet, the presence was there, within arm's reach. I tried to touch it.

Nothing.

It occurred to me to call or visit Xavier or Robin downstairs. But what should I tell them? In times like these, one feels very lonely. I came back to my senses and began to talk to myself. Hearing my own voice reassured me. I calmed down. Eventually the presence dispersed throughout the room. I convinced myself that the origin of the troubles was an overly fertile imagination accompanied by a strong desire to be at home in Marseille with my girlfriend. I was worried about the time wasted not sleeping: two o'clock in the morning already! I never suffered from insomnia though! The need to sleep was getting heavier and heavier. Eyes open, light on, I tried to fall asleep... All I had to do was wait until the next morning...

In the morning, I preferred not to adress the subject with my new colleagues. I had known them only a few days, but the fact that we were living together would allow us to get to know each other more quickly. Sharing this house seemed like a game to us, an opportunity to become teenagers again for a while. They asked me no questions except about the dark circles that were beginning to appear under my eyes. From this point of view, we all three agreed that we had slept very badly, but maybe not for the same reasons?! the subject was not brought up any more. Priority: going to work.

At the end of the day, I went home alone to change my clothes because outside of work hours I liked to be relaxed. We had planned to have dinner in the evening in a pizzeria in "Place de la brèche": the "Villagio".

As soon as the meal was over, all I wanted to do was catch up on my sleep. When I arrived home, I quickly climbed the wooden stairs covered with a rather faded green carpet. But between the first and second floors I felt a shock, I was entering something, losing my balance, as if pushed! My head turned towards the inside of the spiral and my whole body was pushed into the void. I regained consciousness after these fractions of a second, I realized that I had almost fallen into the emptiness of the spiral, but in fact I was alone in the stairwell despite the violence I felt! Fear took hold of me. I immediately went back down to the ground floor and sat down in front of the television. Confused. Once again, I blamed my imagination and fatigue for what had happened. Convinced that it was all my fault, I did not try to find other reasons and take them seriously. This reassured me. "Coué" method effective! Its only drawback is that it does not stop time! Already midnight.

I made a second attempt to reach my room. No difficulty. Thus, began the strangest night I would ever experience...
As soon as I laid down and the lamp was off, the presence reappeared, getting closer and closer. My reaction was similar to that of the previous night. I instinctively pulled the duvet up to my shoulders and left the light on. There was a cold airstream

slipping down my left arm and neck. Then, for the first time, I felt a contact in my neck, a point was slowly penetrating it... The need to stop this pain made me put my right hand on it. The pain faded away... Then it was in my chest with the impression that someone was fumbling inside me, I felt pain in my heart. Violent pain, in crescendo, as if someone wanted to take it away from me. Instinctively I took the foetal position, lying on my left side to protect my heart. My arms protected my chest and the pain in my neck started again! My hands were protecting my neck, the pain in my heart was coming back! Back and forth between pains!

"Go away, I didn't do anything to you, I'm sleepy!" I heard myself say. In vain. To stop the pain, I started pacing around the room. Completely drained, I had the feeling that a part of myself had been stolen, a part of my energy.

I lived like this and despite myself, my second all-nighter.

At breakfast, my two colleagues confessed to me that they had slept very badly again. I tried to question them. Why did you question them? Apart from a certain uneasiness, which they were not used to, they felt nothing else. I found myself alone, faced with the memory of my night scenes, convinced that I was the victim of a much too fertile imagination. At least that is what I kept repeating myself over and over again.

Wednesday, September 3, 1991 around 7:30 p.m. Niort, Deux-Sèvre, France. The evidence appears.

When I got to my room, I would go to the unopened window when I left in the morning. I was bending down to hang one of the two shutters... Suddenly I felt someone rush over me and push me into the void. I had the reflex to turn around and lean against the wall. The presence had reappeared, as my own seemed one too many!

Several months passed before I accepted the idea that I had gone through a totally unexpected and exceptional experience. This realization (or rather this alternative) appeared to me when I slept alone in other places during this same period. Whether it was in Marseille, Paris or Moulins, at friends' houses, at home or in a hotel, skiing, on weekends or on business trips, I never felt this presence anywhere else but in this house. Was it related to the place? Was it related to my psychological state when I was in Niort and was under real pressure due to the workload?

I began to think that this house had a lot to do with it because I had the opportunity to sleep in much gloomier places in Niort as well as other cities, in the "Deux-Sèvres", in other departments, in hotels or in buildings declared historical monuments, in dark alleys, in poorly maintained buildings, with noisy wooden floors where I heard insects, unwanted rodents. But never anything identical!

Does the unknown have to be scary? I do not think it does.

As time went by, this situation appeared to me as a challenge: to get used to living with this presence. This, anyhow, is the reasoning I held between Monday 27 February 1992, the date of my return to Niort, and 11 November 1992, the date of a meeting that was about to change my life.

I refused the evidence again. I remembered the discussions I had had with my parents about the existence of telluric lines. From what I had understood at that time, this phenomenon presented a kind of magnetic net, composed of meshes of about two square meters, present on the entire surface of the earth. When two lines intersect, it forms a knot. It seems to have been proven that it is unhealthy to stay at the level of a knot: putting a bed there can lead to insomnia, for example. Moreover, this net is not always uniform, so it has certain zones with magnetic amplitudes that are more pronounced than others. This explanation suited me perfectly and I decided to remedy this by moving my bed to the other room on the second floor, which is smaller in size. That reassured me!

Change of room.

I asked Xavier to help me move the bed. When I got to the second floor, he asked me about the purpose of this operation. "I don't sleep well in this room, I prefer a smaller room," I replied. He accepted this explanation. We got to work. In a few minutes, everything was transferred to the other room. After he left, I would lie on the bed and watch the room. The fact that the space was smaller gave me confidence. The size of the bed left little room on the sides. The new location was perpendicular to the previous one. The consequences of the first hypothetically badly chosen location in relation to these telluric lines should no longer be felt as before. I laid down, serene.

Unfortunately, the regained tranquillity lasted only for a few moments, as the presence came to visit me like it did on previous nights. But a new kind of cohabitation took place. Never again did I feel violence, aggression, as described above. That same night, the presence appeared near the wooden door, crossed it, carefully avoided the large bed on which I was standing and approached me from the left side. I believe it was at that moment that I promised myself that I would never come back to this house and never sleep there again. I was tired of being subjected to something that I didn't understand and that exhausted me day after day. This is how, every night when I slept in this house, this presence came to me and the pain in my neck appeared. If a small part of my neck was ever poorly protected by my hand, I felt like a long knitting needle slowly going into it. Therefore I felt myself losing a bit of myself, losing a bit of my energy. I had the sensation of emptying myself of something, a sensation totally different from a blood test for example, where you only feel the sting without losing anything.

In my opinion, only two hypotheses remained coherent at that time:
- The lack of well-being linked to this house, caused by the annoyance of finding myself eight hundred kilometres away from home, was playing nasty tricks on me,
- The notion of ghost wasn't just a myth.

There was no evidence at that time to support one hypothesis over another. I was becoming more and more curious, more and more willing to observe and understand these events.

Even though I considered this situation a real challenge, sometimes I was too tired to take up the challenge, some nights I could not put up with it, and went to sleep on the other side of town. Two or three times a month, I would go to a small hotel above a bar where I could find some serenity and sleep soundly all night. Of course, I paid for this hotel at my own expense. It was the price of a good night's sleep!

At that time, I had made friends with an analyst programmer from a service company whose family lived in the area. She had rented a small apartment in old Niort. I spent a few months dating her. Some evenings, I would meet her at her place, so my absences did not seem suspicious or abnormal to my two colleagues.

But curiosity, the will to one day master this phenomenon or, at least understand it better, remained very strong in me. Knowing myself, I think that if I had tried to permanently change my accommodation, I would have regretted it later and would have reproached myself for not having stubbornly sought answers to my questions.

These phenomena that have triggered in me this thirst to find answers to the fundamental questions that everyone must ask themselves one day or another:

- What is life?
- What is our role on earth?
- What is death?
- When does life end?
- What is the function of religions?
- How would I react to the death of a loved one?
- What is spirit?
- What happens to the spirit when the body envelope disappears?
- And finally, when does a human being turn into a ghost?

I had been confronted with the deaths of my grandparents ten years earlier, but I was not yet ripe for these issues. I accepted the facts in a fatal way, like any individual who loses a loved one without having the intelligent need to answer the question "why?

The period from September to December 1991 was the most terrible period. It was impossible for me to be alone in the house. I made sure that it was not the case, I left Niort every weekend and accepted every possible invitation. All my curiosity was no longer enough, I was afraid of the possible psychological and physical consequences.

My main alternative was to sleep in this small hotel in Niort. We would enter it through the bar and then go upstairs to the rooms. I only went there to sleep. In the morning I would go back to the villa to take a shower and get my things for work. It wasn't very expensive, but it still pissed me off to pay for the hotel when my employer rented a large, spacious mansion with outbuildings. But it was indispensable because I broke down morally from time to time. I was very tired and exhausted by my work. These nights allowed me to recharge my batteries and get back to work for the rest of the week.

Wednesday, December 25, 1991. Marseille, Bouches du Rhône, France. My false liberation.

In November 1991, I filed a request for a one-month paid leave covering the holiday season and the beginning of January 1992. At the same time, I asked the people in charge of the "Société de Services et de Conseils" to change my contract in order for me to stay in the Marseille region as soon as my leave was over, despite my interest in the project I was working on.

To my great surprise, my application was accepted without much questioning since my hiring had been made on the condition that I would one day work in the Marseille region. This had not been the case for two years.

I therefore organized my departure to the client (MACIF) by inviting my entourage to a farewell drink as was customary in the department at that time, and warmly thanked the Head of Studies of the MACIF's Information Systems Department for his trust for six months. I was asked very few delicate questions, I was leaving for personal reasons with other contracts.

All my personal belongings were moved to Marseille with my personal 205 Peugeot. As soon as I came back from my holidays, my employer told me that there were no new projects. In order to avoid inter-contracting, I provided two training courses in office automation on EXCEL and WORD software to a group of secretaries in a small business in the Paluds industrial zone near the town of Gémenos.

The end of year 1991 holidays was spent without being on the roads of France with my family on December 25th without having to take a train or my car the next day or on the very night.

At the beginning of 1992, as the situation was not improving in terms of new contracts, I found myself at the Marseille agency for a few weeks without activity. On the other hand, the manager of the Atlantic agency was still looking for someone to replace me and would gladly accept me back if I wanted. It was difficult for me to refuse this unique proposal and so I found myself, again, at the end of February 1992 on the road towards Deux-Sèvres with all my personal belongings.

I moved back into the same room on the second floor of the villa in the presence of my two Parisian colleagues Xavier and Robin. After a month of great depression, a real cohabitation with the ghost took place.

Here are some anecdotes that I still remember...

I always avoided sleeping alone in this house; however, we would frequently expect each other at home after work, as we all had different work constraints. I remember one evening sitting alone in front of the television in the living room on the ground floor. The 8:30 p.m. film was well underway when I heard the kitchen front door open and close suddenly. This door was made of an iron frame with tiles like those usually found in verandas. Then, I heard footsteps going through the kitchen. This room resonated a lot and the noises reminded me of Robin's in his moments of intense fatigue, satisfied to have finished a day's work. "Robin, do you want to go out to dinner in the city? "I asked. The sound of footsteps came closer to the entrance of the living room... The walk was slow but firm and sounded just like Robin's. I heard the person put his parka on the coat rack at the bottom of the spiral staircase. Hearing no answer, I got up from the couch and went to meet Robin... to realize that I was still alone in the house! This experience occurred several times again. Every time, there was no doubt in my mind that I was hearing a physical person coming.

One evening, we went out for a drink in one of the two lively bars in Niort and then returned home at around one o'clock in the morning and quickly return to our respective rooms. After I went to bed, I heard a person climbing the spiral staircase with a determined step between the first and second floors. The footsteps stopped in front of my bedroom door. We often had instructions to pass on to each other for the next day; I naturally thought that one of my colleagues was about to knock on the door. But no more noise. So, I got up to meet him, opened the bedroom door, and realized that I was alone. Convinced that the noise was real, I went down to the first floor to check if my two colleagues were in their room. And they were. Confused, I went back up in mine...

In the winter, the house was heated by electric convectors. One of them was installed at the base of my bedroom window. I had noticed many times that, when the ghost passed to the right of my bed, that is to say, to the side of the window, the passage being narrow, barely one foot, the thermostat also detected the cold airstream of the ghost, and I could hear the sound of the heater being turned on. Sometimes in the evening, I would have fun trying to anticipate the thermostat's click according to my evaluation of its movement. With a margin of error of one second, I was able to identify when the thermostat was going to go off. Every time, this detail pleased me because it confirmed that I was not dreaming, that this phenomenon was real and not fabricated by my imagination. A few seconds later, I could feel the cold airstream on my hand or on my arm on the side where the entity wandered. And ultimately, the pain in my neck began. With time, this pain was getting better, but I still had the unpleasant feeling that a part of my being was being stolen from me without really being able to avoid it.

The presence was also accompanied by tiny ringing in the ears not comparable to the tinnitus generated in a nightclub, for example. The difference was that this noise came from outside of my head and was not generated by the ear itself.

It came from the front door in ninety-five percent of the time and moved slowly or, more precisely, I never observed any sudden movements on its part.

Sometimes, when the entity arrived, I sat on my bed to better observe the phenomenon. With the light off, I could sometimes distinguish a discreet humanoid form moving around. Only the contours were noticeable, the inside of the form only slightly modified the perception of the background. The results were similar to the distortion of a low magnification magnifying glass. Each time, I could see the shape of a bearded man, dressed like people in the Middle Ages, wearing some sort of toga.

Another detail had intrigued me: my bed was positioned against the wall at head level. Sometimes the entity went around the bed by passing along the wall. This way, it managed to stay on the second floor without considering the vertical elements of the house, namely the doors and the walls. This complete tour of the bed reminded me of an exhibition of two events in one place: me, in my bed, and the entity. However, I never observed the entity passing through the floor between the second floor and the first floor. But it does not mean it could not do it.

During the second part of the stay, I was decided to bring a camera to see the possible marks that this entity could leave on a film, even if the light halo was extremely weak but without any conviction that it would appear on the photo. I prepared, on many occasions, my 24 x 36 in Marseille to take it with me. And yes, at that time, we did not all have a mobile phone that allowed us to instantly share any exceptional situation! But only the ending of this story came unexpectedly cutting short any possibility to do so! Indeed, I thought I had time to do it but eventually, I did not. I regret it of course!

Later, I had the opportunity to discuss it with my two colleagues, they confirmed their discomfort in this house but told me that they did not feel this presence as much as I did.

During this period, Jean, our manager, hired a saleswoman. Arriving from another region, he offered her temporary accommodation in the house before she found a place to live. Having learned the news, we decided not to tell her anything about the house to see how she would react. On the evening of her arrival, she moved to the second floor in the large bedroom. We wished her a good night. The next morning, we met for breakfast. She came down last, which intensified our impatience to see her. Eventually, she arrived, with shadows under her eyes and said:

- I slept so badly last night!

Of course, we laughed and told her how we had felt since our arrival. This house made everyone I knew at that time feel uncomfortable. There were, however, differences in feelings.

Everyone in this house admitted to hearing strange noises, feeling uncomfortable and having had severe insomnia. The tiredness accumulated there was greater than anywhere else for the same work. However, none of the consultants lived in this house full time. What would it have been like if this had been the case?!

Wednesday, November 11, 1992. Niort, Deux-Sèvres, France. Confirmation of the evidence.

Proposing a public holiday to celebrate Armistice Day is an excellent initiative that no one will contradict. But for people on business trip, these holidays only matter if they happen to be on a Monday or Friday, otherwise it is impossible to go home for a single day! Therefore, it is often an opportunity to visit the local region. This time, the weather was not suitable: a storm had raged throughout the night from Tuesday to Wednesday. I got up several times to hang up the shutters to prevent them from flapping all night long. It was unpleasant to say the least, especially in a haunted house!

However, I enjoyed being able to stay under my duvet all morning and laze around until mid-afternoon. I then decided to visit a colleague at work, Elise B. from Nantes. When I arrived, she was not alone at home. Myleene, one of her friends from Nantes was visiting her. They had planned to have dinner together and proposed me to join them. I gladly accepted. We left for the restaurant.

In the conversation, Elise mentioned to the storm of the previous night. Knowing the situation in the house, she smiled complacently at me and asked me how the night had gone. I replied that it had been nothing more than a very noisy night due to the storm. Myleene asked for more explanation for these innuendoes. Elise spoke up and apologized to her friend for not informing her earlier, especially since she was a psychic. A long dialogue began between the two of us about the haunted house. I had my first esotericism class as a neophyte that I was.

Elise was listening sceptically. This topic did not seem to be part of their usual conversations. A table had been reserved in the Turkish restaurant near the dungeon on the banks of the river "Sèvre niortaise". Throughout the meal, the discussion was very lively. When it was time for dessert, Myleene took a sheet of paper and asked me to draw the rooms of the house on it. I represented the ground floor, kitchen, living room, fireplace, staircase, outbuildings, stable... Then, Myleene, without knowing the function of these rooms, took out two coloured pens and began to concentrate. Using the pens, Myleene added, with precision, two dots of blue colour, symbol of water: one to the left of the front door and the other in front of the front door in the first room. She asked me what these dots could correspond to. I could not find anything to answer. To her, these points could represent taps or concentrations of pipes. With this additional information, I answered her: the second point was the location of the sink in the kitchen but the first one was not corresponding to anything.

She then completed the drawing with two red circles, specifying that these two locations should be avoided. The first was located at the entrance to the outbuildings at the circuit breaker level and the second on the left of the kitchen, in place of a table that we never used. I noticed, without mentioning it, that the installation of my bed when I arrived in the house was vertical from this point on the second floor.

Myleene plunged her hand into her bag and looked at us satisfied: "I always carry a pendulum with me! ». She took out of her bag a small ball hanging on a wire. "We can go to this house tonight," she added. I did not feel any anxiety, but rather a kind of relief. Maybe I can get to the bottom of what has been going on in this house for a year! We paid the bill. Direction: "impasse des épinettes"!

I parked in the courtyard. I had barely opened the front door of the house that Myleene was already looking for something behind the lavender sheaves hanging along the wall...
"Gilles, there is indeed something to the left of the door! "Myleene said proudly. Indeed, behind the lavender sheaves was a tap! I was the first to be surprised, I had never noticed it. But it was only the beginning of a long list of surprises...

Myleene suggested that we make a first tour of the rooms to observe the behaviour of her pendulum. She began to move, at awfully slow steps, in the different rooms. The pendulum confirmed the red dot drawn in the kitchen by a slight inclination and rotation on itself. The ground floor rooms did not reveal anything more: the pendulum swung slightly but without any significant angle. The same occurred for the first floor. On the second floor, I invited the two friends to enter the large room in which I had originally settled. To my surprise, the pendulum kept a reasonable angle.

We had gone around the house, there was nothing significant. Myleene offered to go around the house again. Nothing more. But on the second floor, Myleene noticed a closed door on the landing. "What's behind it?" she asked me. "A storage room," I replied, surprised I had not thought of it myself. Since we never went there, I had not thought to mention this tiny room of only 1.5 square meters. Myleene offered to let us in. In the middle was a pile of old chairs and many cobwebs! Only one person could enter, just by standing on the threshold. Myleene entered with the pendulum. As soon as she arrived, the pendulum rotated horizontally with great speed. It was the first time I had seen a pendulum move so much. The most surprising thing was that it began to rotate without initiating kinetic energy, i.e. without taking up speed: it seemed to have acquired it instantly. As a good sceptic person, it seemed totally impossible to me to position this pendulum horizontally with a movement of the hand. Especially since it kept this angle for five to eight seconds without any weakness or drop in speed.

Myleene turned her head towards us: "There's something weird in this room! ». Elise and I watched astounded at the pendulum. Elise, nervous, had hysterical laughter. Personally, I was beginning to become aware of the rare and exceptional situation I was living in.

Myleene came out of the storeroom to go around the last room not visited during the second passage: my bedroom. The pendulum then began to rotate at a slight angle, close to vertical. Myleene wanted to study the case of the storage room again and entered it again. But this time the pendulum did not show any particular agitation. Myleene turned back to us and said in a firm tone: "The thing has disappeared... or has moved since then! ».

Please believe that this scene will remain engraved in my memory for the rest of my life! Not only had I never seen the use of a pendulum before, but to see a link between a pendulum as a material object and a ghost-like phenomenon can be perplexing. This must have been the first anguish of the evening...
Myleene suggested that we get in touch with these possible entities. We went into the living room. Myleene needed an object to serve as an intermediary or interface, a tool to establish communication with the afterlife. She took a folding chair (!) and put both hands on the front of the pedestal. Myleene sat on the

couch and began to concentrate. Elise sat across from Myleene on a chair on the other side of the room, I sat on the right side of Myleene, facing the front door. We formed a triangle, so that we could observe each other.

Elise let out some convulsive laughter. I think she had difficulty believing the scene she was experiencing. It did seem a bit zany to see a person holding a folding chair as a mean of communication with the afterlife! For my part, I was very troubled as I became more and more aware of the situation. I no longer had to question myself, the origin of all this was not a personal psychological situation but a haunted house with entities!

About ten minutes of silence passed...

Myleene's chair began to move back and forth, in small irregular jolts, but for me, nothing significant.

After a few tens of seconds, I began to feel the same ringing in my ears as on previous evenings... A presence appeared, went through the wide-open front door of the living room and moved towards Myleene. As it passed by, I felt a well-defined cold airstream on my left arm, the side closest to Myleene. I felt the same presence as the previous days. I started to become really aware of the experience I had lived in the previous months: it was not my fault, not a heart or psychological problem linked to my remoteness, not a problem of tiredness linked to my sustained work, but a real physical phenomenon that managed to interact with its environment. I was amazed. I was waiting for confirmation from the psychic, which was about to come.

Myleene spoke: "I am in contact with an entity, it is in front of me, in the room." I had the absolute certainty, shared with the feeling of that moment, that I had experienced something supernatural in the previous months.

We did not ask her any questions at that time. We were too disturbed by what was going on. We were past any classical situation, past any school teaching, past any religious beliefs. This type of experience is extremely destabilizing. The impression of jumping into the unknown, with no frame of reference, no past to fall back on. A good point, though, this time there were three of us experiencing the same thing. It was a little more reassuring!

A few moments later, Myleene came out of her state of high concentration to inform us of the situation:
- It's over for this entity, it's joined other spheres. But it's not over.
- Why? Are there others? I asked.
- Yes, she answered, there are three entities attached to this house, I will then release the other two.
- Can you explain this phenomenon to us?
- At the moment of passing into the Hereafter, what we call death or physical death of the person, when the astral body leaves its shell, things do not always go well. That is often the case with people who are too materialistic. Here we are dealing with people who have suffered violent deaths; it seems that this dates to the Hundred Years' War; they have remained attached to the place of their sacrifice, that is to say, this house.

Myleene concentrated again. This happened twice as she had indicated before.
- I will ask my guide if there are no more entities, she said.
A few minutes later, she gave us the answer:
- There are other entities.
- Did you get the number wrong? I asked ironically.

- Not at all, she said, these other entities are not attached to the house but to the place only. There are many of them, so I will help them to reach the spheres more suitable for their condition.

Myleene concentrated again, hands on the chair. I did not feel anything during those few minutes, yet Myleene concluded:
- I asked them to give you back your energy, she said, then a few seconds later added:
- It's over, there are no more entities attached here. Gilles, you shouldn't be embarrassed anymore, she said.
A little sceptical about this quick conclusion, I replied anyway:
- I fully hope, the end of tonight and the next nights will bring the answer.
- Are you sure you can sleep here tonight? Elise asked me.

Elise was right, after the experience of that evening, the night in this place would not be easy! But fortunately, I no longer felt anguish, rather relief and growing curiosity, I had my answer but I had to confirm it. "The challenge is interesting! You have to know if it worked or not! ». So, I walked the two girls back to their car and promised to tell them what would happen the next morning.

Back home, I found myself alone in the house again, as my two colleagues had planned to return from Paris the next morning. A real uneasiness persisted still, but I went straight to my room and closed the door. I decided to turn off the light, but I was very agitated and could not sleep. A few minutes later I felt a presence at the entrance of the room, perhaps less marked than the other times.

I thought Mylene was wrong. What is going on? The entity bypassed the bed, just like the other times to get close to my face. I saw inside of me like a luminous veil. My first reaction was to turn on the bedside lamp. There was no change. "Go away, I'm sleepy!" I was especially disappointed by the mistake Myleene made. To my surprise, the entity disappeared without my neck hurting at all. The rest of the night was quiet, but I could not regain my calm.

The next day, I told Elise about the event. Overloaded with work, I entrusted Elise with the task to let Myleene know about the night I had spent. She did not have an answer, she only offered to come back next time. Eventually, the following nights turned out to be serene without any presence like the previous months. The phenomenon had disappeared over the days thanks to Myleene, the house was no longer haunted.

To say that we felt good in this house would have been a bit optimistic! It is hard to cope with a year of anguish like the one I went through. As soon as I entered this house, I always had an anxiety attack, just like when I turned off the light in my room. As I fell asleep, I would listen for all the strange noises as I checked the whole room, waiting for something or someone. I felt less tired, but it did not seem significant to me. I thought this story was over, but I was wrong...

Wednesday, January 6, 1993. Niort, Deux-Sèvres, France. The epilogue of this adventure.

The launch of the new MACIF information system took place as planned at the beginning of the year. We were then entering the computer maintenance phase of the project. Jean told us that our contracts were being renewed every week, my departure was imminent. We had set up a three-eight working mode, in order to be able to absorb the fluctuating correction workload due to incidents or anomalies detected by users in the various regions of MACIF and by the various regional IT teams. Xavier had taken a few days of forced leave: one of his relatives had gone into hospital for serious issues. Only Robin and I were present in the house.

On Friday, January 15, 1993, Jean informed me that my contract ended at the end of the week, i.e. Sunday, January 17. He wanted me to work the next day, Saturday, teaming with Robin. I accepted and thus planned to return to Marseille on Sunday during the day.

On Friday night, I experienced the same phenomenon as before: an entity was in my room. At first my feelings were the same as before Myleene's intervention, but without neck pain, there was only a bright haze of light inside my body. I turned on the bedside lamp to reassure myself. But the haze persisted, the vision of the room was in the background. I didn't feel any pain, I just had the impression that I was sharing my body with someone else: the spirit that I had liberated had fit into my body!

Then I heard words from inside of me. They were words of peace, serenity, and appreciation. The entity was telling me that this was my last night in this house. It came to thank me for helping it reach the present spheres. I did not need to speak, we understood each other as if we were connected, my feelings were shared without any effort to articulate, to construct a sentence, to decode an auditory flow, everything was natural. Then the mind simply left just as it had come. This scene seemingly lasted a few minutes. But I am not sure, the time seemed different.

How can the entity contradict the directives of my manager? Wasn't I supposed to work the next day, Saturday, with Robin, and sleep the night of Saturday in this house to leave for Marseille, Sunday? This detail troubled me very much, all night long. Saturday morning, we went to work very early as agreed with Jean, curious to see what would happen during that day.

When we arrived, Jean was assessing the incidents that had occurred during the night to correct them, and the load generated. Jean turned to us and told us that he had overestimated the workload, our interventions were not justified. "It turns out you can take the weekend off!" he concluded with a big smile.

Robin decided to go straight back to Paris. I found myself alone, with a free weekend, facing a true dilemma: return to Marseille and consequently confirm what the entity said? Or to remain a little more in Niort and thus prove that I remained master of myself? What to decide? The temptation to stay was strong, I had such a feeling of no longer being myself, that I was no longer the master of my destiny! But at that moment, I knew that everything was still possible: I only had to decide. Staying one more day would only serve to show that the entity was wrong, but I was wasting a weekend that I could have spent with my loved ones. I knew I could do it: what more could I get out of it? Going home to Marseille meant simplicity, it brought me happiness and serenity. It was the most obvious decision I would have made spontaneously if the entity had not told me in advance! I would not have hesitated for a second!
Very tormented by this last experience, I still decided to prepare my things and return to Marseille the same day. Even though I was burning with envy to stay one more day, the happiness of returning home, seeing my loved ones and my house was stronger. This last solution, obviously, took the upper hand. And then, I admit, this story was becoming too heavy, too burdensome, I was longing to move on, to simply live my life.

That is how this story ended. I never saw John, Robin, Elise, and Myleene again. I regret it, it would have been interesting to hear their vision of the events, especially Myleene. As for Xavier, I had the opportunity to see him much later, in the Paris region, without really speaking again about this period in Niort, but more generally about more recent events and the consequences of our respective divorces. Our common memories were mainly drunk nights spent together with Robin in the various restaurants in Niort that we had the opportunity to try during this year of mobility.

A few years later, social networks allowed me to virtually reconnect with Xavier, I then found the trace of Robin. Then, the one of Jean, who was hired at MACIF after the project and who then moved to the Paris region as an independent consultant. I never saw the band again.

In August 2014, despite my research, I did not find any trace of Elise or Myleene. A new search in January 2019 allowed me to find Elise who had no contact with Myleene since her divorce.

This part was written from notes taken shortly after the fact, telling me that it would be regrettable to forget all these events. Despite moving a lot, I never lost these sheets. I have had the opportunity to share this experience with many people who have always been questioning, concerned or even interested in this exceptional adventure. It is especially its ending that allowed me to reflect on our human destiny.

My reflections on destiny started from this experience and made me understand that it is better to listen to oneself in order to optimize one's freedom to act or rather to interact during one's entire earthly life. This is my intimate conviction.

Therefore, I decided to share my experience with more people as well as my reflections on Life that have been maturing in me for more than twenty years. This is a fascinating subject, but as it stands, I can only share my intimate convictions since science does not bring any element. The strong point of my reflections is that they are based on an experience lived during more than a year. Therefore, it is not a philosophical book. Everyone can make their own ideas. Also, let us not forget that our hectic lives, take us away too often from the most important foundations of an earthly life, where we will all be concerned by death, one day or another.

« *Knowledge is gained through experience,*
Everything else is just information. »
Albert Einstein

Testimony of Xavier F.

I proposed to Xavier F. to write a text on the common professional period in Niort. I am sending it to you as it was given to me. Xavier does not go into details as I do, he only relates his memories, written more than twenty-five years after the events!

Let me introduce myself: Xavier F., one of the three consultants who lived in this house during the M.A.C.I.F. information system redesign project. Freshly graduated from the French school EPITA (Ecole Pour l'Informatique et les Techniques Avancées) computer school in Paris, I was hired by a small computer consulting firm. This human-sized structure was working on big IT projects, the atmosphere was really pleasant and that's what convinced me.

The first contacts with the managers of this structure allowed me to create bonds of trust and to feel motivated to launch myself into the adventure. At that time, the consultant structures were developing exponentially and this one had all the potential to do so. So, I accepted the offer with pleasure, ready to invest myself totally in it.

The first proposed mission was in Niort in a large mutual insurance company: the M.A.C.I.F.

Being single and without constraints, I accepted this offer with the possibility of going home every weekend with my personal car, especially since my Audi A4, newly bought, allowed me to make the trip in less than three and a half hours! I loved to drive, often at night with "the feeling of a sailor sailing from port to port", the lights of the villages reminding me of civilization and, subject to using my radar detector forbidden in France but bought during my last trip to the United States.

Another Parisian was introduced to me to complete the necessary team at the client's site: Robin P., a consultant slightly older than me and already having a little experience in the consulting field where the essential thing is not technical knowledge of technologies but rather human relations! I proposed him to drive in my car, which would allow us to get to know each other better and to share unique and very friendly moments of life!

When we arrived in Niort, we met the director of the Northeast subsidiary, Jean D., who was very upset to receive us. He introduced us to the project and our respective roles within the M.A.C.I.F. He then offered to accommodate us, with a third consultant, in a house in Niort, an offer we accepted without hesitation. From that moment on, I was imagining the nights out I was going to make with my new friends!

I was meeting Elise B. and Gilles B. at an internal meeting at the consulting firm. All of us clicked very quickly. As a young C... graduate, a bit presumptuous without realizing it, I lived the narcissistic certainties of my performance as a universal truth. I never had any doubts. I was all the more at ease as the team around me was much more experienced than I was in the field and that, without saying it or making me feel it, they forgave me my ardour, my impetuosity, in short my latent immaturity and the youth that I could sometimes show.

I was involved in the choice of our future housing. We had visited three houses in the presence of Jean D., our manager and Fabienne, the organizing secretary of this race, after the day's work. We left earlier than usual for this event. The selected house was spacious, and the parking lot allowed us to park our three cars. On the other hand, this old building was very dark and rather gloomy.

It was not really the house of our dreams, but it was a pied-à-terre near the workplace as Jean reminded us so well! Moreover, we had no trouble projecting the full potential of freedom and possible parties since it had no immediate neighbourhood!

As soon as the decision was made, Robin moved to the largest room on the first floor. After discussion with Gilles, I took the other room on the first floor near the bathroom. If I had to caricature the situation, I would say that I was the impetuous navel-gazing joker, Robin the big party boy and Gilles the quiet force of observation, thought and moderation.

From the first breakfast, we shared our difficulty in finding sleep on that first night. But there was nothing exceptional. It was the recurring difficulty of sleeping peacefully that was troubling.

I also remember the arrival of the new saleswoman who stayed for one night on the second floor. We had agreed not to tell her anything when she arrived and to wait for her reaction to this house. We had a good laugh when we shared her feeling the first morning at breakfast: she had slept badly!

Gilles shared his experience with us a few weeks after our installation. However, our investment in our consulting missions meant that we had never dwelt on this type of subject before. I remember one time when I was in the bathroom, alone in the house, I heard strange noises that did not worry me particularly. At first I was far from being interested in what was subjective and not explained by science, then, this house, was above all for me a dormitory or a bachelor flat, we never ate there and we were not there during the day. Indeed, on weekends and holidays, my priority was to return home, to see some of my conquests again until Niort absorbed me completely to the point of rooting me there for love.

Finally, I notice today that I have gradually left this house, to live intensely my "local love". A new feeling emerging today with a question: was it only the passion that unconsciously guided me in this escape or this "strange" and "bizarre" house that pushed me to forget my friends there to the point of abandoning them?

My memories are limited to the evenings at the restaurant between consultants, our few well drunk evenings with Robin when Gilles was going to join his girlfriend, my love affairs then my great love for a woman and a superb national computer project.

After this period in Niort, I returned to the Paris region and worked for other clients of the consulting firm. I lost contact with Robin and Elise. My career in the field of information systems allowed me to work for large international groups such as Oracle.

Gilles and I regularly shared our common concerns and life paths, especially during our respective divorces. This is how I became more mature and how the real issues of life brought us closer together. I think so.

Catholic by family tradition, having become an atheist, I became a believer again at the age of forty, even though everything was going well. Indeed, churches attracted me more and more like a magnet and one day I decided not to fight anymore. My spirituality helps me today to conceive life differently with much more humanity, understanding, listening and attention for others. It also helps me in my fight against cancer, which I sincerely experience as "*an evil for a good*". It has led me to discover who I am deeply.

Second part

My deductions, the basis of my demonstration

« It's in absolute ignorance of our raison d'être which is the root of our sadness and disgust. »

Anatole France, The Garden of Epicure, 1894

The purpose of this second part is to detail certain concepts. Therefore, the change of style is radical.

My approach is systemic, and I also borrow its vocabulary (system, interact, interrelate, process, ...). Thus, I consider concepts as abstract systems. But I will not attempt to detail the functioning of a mind or a ghost: these are "systems" far too complex for my level of knowledge. The chosen methodology: choose a term, recall its definition from the online dictionary larousse.fr, link it with my experience in Niort by developing an empirical approach, then develop my theory based on my deep conviction, my experience, my discussions and my few readings, and finally propose a new definition. Some people will recognize religious principles in it, particularly elements of Buddhist principles. As for those who would be hermetic to these principles and too far from current dogmas, I invite them to ask themselves the following questions: "What interest did I have in spending so much time and research for such an incredible story? A story that will bring me nothing except the risk of making a fool of myself? ». But it is a pleasure for me to share an extraordinary story with you in the true sense of the word.

> « *Every truth goes through three stages:*
> *First, it's ridiculed.*
> *Second, it is violently opposed.*
> *Third, it is accepted as being self-evident.* »
> Arthur Schopenhauer, German philosopher

My way of interacting with you has been writing this book. So I thank you in advance for your indulgence because I know there will be mistakes. There will be room for improvement, perhaps to make new editions? On this subject, working by iterations seems appropriate to me.

In any case, I am extremely interested in the numerous and constructive exchanges that could emerge after reading the book!

In this part, a chapter is dedicated to the notion of spirit. But to make it easier to read, I anticipate this point by specifying that I only talk about spirit in this book because I consider that the soul is an integral part of the mind and serves as an interface between mind and body. This "module" of the spirit has therefore no reason to exist outside of an earthly life.

Even if the subject is dealt with as seriously as possible, based on numerous researches and reflections shared with people from very diverse backgrounds, I always keep in mind the quote from the French humourist and comedian Pierre Dac: "*Forecasting is difficult, especially when it concerns the future*".

Let us remain humble before this subject which seeks to understand if life has a meaning. Destiny remains linked to the future of humanity, and this will remain a central topic for a long time to come.

Ghosts: a situation between two dimensions

Dictionary definition: Appearance of a deceased person as a real being[2]

I have no doubt about it: the phenomenon exists! But we are in a special case. Death must allow us to "change state" quickly to change dimension. Consequently, life continues after death. There is a Life beyond earthly life.

In the observed case, this "in-between" state is experienced by the deceased. This was brought to me when it thanked me during the last night in this house. This ghost only wanted to reach his sphere, but he could not do it alone. It took the help of a medium to complete this step.

We can interact with a ghost, but in a limited way. We can observe its effects on matter, we can exchange energy. We manage to communicate with it, even if my experience is not obvious on this point, since the real communication obtained was with the entity having joined its sphere and not with the "ghost". However, the medium did obtain communication. Also, we can help a ghost to reach its dimension and complete its "change of state". This is an important point.

A ghost is an individual in its own right, autonomous, reflective and it needs energy. It modifies the space it uses, concretized by a difference in temperature. It is colder around the ghost than elsewhere in the room. The delimitation of the ghost, its boundary in the systemic sense, is very precise, similar to an envelope delimited by the image of its clothes when it is not

---

[2] Definitions from the Larousse.fr online dictionary, Editions Larousse. I thank Editions Larousse for their agreement.

moving. Its movements are smooth and sometimes accompanied by a cold airstream. This space is accompanied by a more or less pronounced luminous halo. Its clothes seem to be those worn at the time of its death. In the case I experienced, there was no trace of injury on it. Last observation: it may also be accompanied by a tiny sound phenomenon, especially audible when the environment is perfectly silent. This is not comparable to tinnitus, but rather to the feeling you get when you are near a power line in wet, rainy weather.

The ghost manages to pass through matter like doors or walls, which I have seen many times. It preferred to pass through an open door rather than a wall, it would go around the bed to get close to me. It must see the room as we see it. It walks on the same floor as we do. This point is strange because it seems to be under the effects of gravity while being able to pass through material elements. This seems impossible, because it is in complete contradiction with Newton's second law called "the fundamental principle of dynamics", that of action-reaction: if they walk, it is because they exert a force on the floor, whereas if they pass through walls, it is because they do not exert any force, and the two are not compatible[3]. It seems to me that the use of the verb "to walk" may not be appropriate, it would be better to say "to float" according to my observations. Perhaps it benefits, for example, from the characteristics of superconductors[4] ? or even a supersolid [5] ?

---

[3] Physicist Costas Efthimiou, from the University of Central Florida (UCF), has decided to use the weapons of physics and mathematics to dismantle some stubborn beliefs: ghosts cannot walk and pass through walls.

[4] This is the case of the Japanese train named Maglev for Magnetic levitation which remains in magnetic levitation thanks to the characteristics of a material that has become superconducting

[5] A supersolid corresponds to a solid at very low temperature (close to absolute zero, i.e. -273.15°C) in which a fraction of a solid body would flow

The three states of matter: solid, liquid, gaseous are taught in school. It seems that other states can emerge when we are close to absolute zero[6]. At least that is what current quantum physics shows. We were not close to absolute zero indeed, but it must be said that my observation has the characteristics of a supersolid: shape and volume are defined, this matter passes through other matter. In such a solid, the atoms are in fact so little linked to each other, that this fundamentally quantum phenomenon can manifest itself.

It would come at night, once I was in my bed. Can we talk about established habits? That makes me believe that he shared the same notion of time as I did, because he never came twice in the same day to take my energy.

It always appeared to me at night or in the evening and was in the second-floor's closet. Did the ghost avoid daylight? What antagonism could there be between a ghost and the energy of the sun? Heat comes from the agitation of atoms. Maybe a ghost is trying to maintain a low temperature? Perhaps it can take advantage of the characteristics of superconductors?

The tiny luminous halo, this cottony atmosphere that surrounds the ghost makes me say that it is still made of atoms. Is the difference between a ghost and a spirit weight-related? The theory of the 21 grams corresponding to the mass of the soul at the time of death (Theory of the American doctor Duncan MacDougall published in the New York Times and the journal American Medicine in March 1907) is less than the difference in

---

through the rest of the solid like a superfluid, i.e. without friction or energy dissipation. www.futura-sciences.com

[6] On the scale of degrees Celsius it is exactly -273.15 °C by convention. This is the lowest temperature allowed by physics

mass calculated when leaving the body: 45 grams (the officials of the Swiss Institute of Notic Sciences ISSNOE, conducted a whole series of different experiments on a young Frenchman who assures to be able to leave his body). But these experiments are based on samples that are too small to be considered a scientific result. However, we find psychostasy, the ceremony of weighing the soul, in many religions such as Nazism, Christianity, Islam, ...and in India, Japan, Tibet, Ancient Egypt. It seals the deceased to an Endless Life or rebirth on earth. It is an interesting line of study because it could explain the difference between a spirit that has managed to reach its sphere and the ghost still attached to our material world. The ghost, which could be considered as a phenomenon close to an exit from the body, contains too many atoms to detach itself from our world and thus change its state.

At the moment of our death, our envelope frees our spirit, which regains its timeless dimension. When this change of state malfunctions, the mind is not totally freed, which prevents it from regaining part of its dimension while remaining in our space-time. This intermediate state is not wanted and is not desirable for the being who goes through it: it can no longer really interact without benefiting from the advantages of the sphere he was supposed to join. This situation between two states seems to me like a jail. The ghost situation is suffered. Can an external interaction help it find the desired target state or can it do it on its own, with a lot of time?

Being always linked to the earthly world, it needs energy so it "steals" it from other living beings. Why use such a strong term? Quite simply because our energy is our capital which is essential for us to live well. Losing it can generate disturbances for the human being over time. The ghost absorbs energy unduly, knowingly by damaging the earthly body. It is a predator despite itself.

I deduce that life on earth is a personal experience. This ghost found itself in this situation, facing this problem alone. I did not see any other entities wanting to help it. During the first contacts, I felt its hatred for human beings, but this situation has calmed down over time. A ghost keeps its character and the image of its clothes. He also keeps a limited ability to interact with other living beings. This is the reason why I compare this situation to a prison, because being on earth without interacting must be horrible if we consider, as I did, that this is the purpose of our existence on earth!

In the case of my experiment in Niort, these entities were only slightly visible in the form of luminous halos. But they contained an area that was colder than the ambient temperature in any season and were very well shaped in terms of the space used. It seems to vary. Some light halos may be much more visible than others, hence the notion of ghosts, so we can clearly see the person as it was at the time of its death, the spirit immersing itself with the shape of the envelope in which it was. Why are clothes considered? It seems to me that everything that is in contact with our body is "taken into account", as if they were enclosed in our energy envelope.

Water seems to facilitate the materialization of these lost spirits. Wet regions and countries where it often rain have many more legends, events, or facts of this type. A place with an underground river will also facilitate these contacts or appearances.

The history of the place is also important. It is believed that those who have suffered wars, or many violent deaths possess many entities. This situation seems bad to me because it generates a lot of interference between our world and the entities. The beings living on earth should be able to find serenity and live fully their state. This is not always possible if the number of entities is too large. Just think of the many haunted, cursed, or strange places referring to historical battle sites to convince us. This is the case of Niort. During the Hundred Years' War the population was massacred by the English and then freed in 1372 by Bertrand Du Guesclin.

I wondered if other people had had the same type of experience with energy removal. I could not find anything except the 10% of French people who say they have felt the presence of a ghost before (article in "science et vie"[7]). However, the characteristics described are close to the legends of vampires, which have their origins in very ancient and diverse mythological traditions: Cain, the second son of Adam and Eve, condemned to exile by God for killing his brother Abel, is said to be the first known vampire. Depending on the region and the period, this monster is described as sucking the blood but also the vital energy of its victims according to the encyclopaedia of the paranormal[8]. Predatory and immortal, condemned to wander. In my experience, the process was identical and daily: two stings pointing downwards at the base of the neck, on either side, which left no trace. Constant fatigue and the feeling of emptying myself, at that very moment, proved to be energy-related.

Based on my experience, I wondered if it was possible that the incarnation of the spirit at the moment of birth could go wrong. There must be some cases where the spirit has difficulty

---

[7] The paranormal deciphered by science, https://www.science-et-vie.com/archives/fantome-voyance-sortie-de-corps-vous-avez-dit-bizarre-9-experiences-paranormales-32050

[8] http://www.paranormal-encyclopedie.com/wiki/Articles/Vampire

integrating the foetus, resulting in the death of the foetus. These failed births must be quite common since there are about 2.6 million stillborn babies a year, half of them at the time of delivery. Of course, many of them could be avoided with better monitoring of pregnancies but in 39% of cases, foetal death remains unexplained, says RHEOP[9].

Proposed definition of a ghost: a living dead still related to material elements.

---

[9] RHEOP : Child Disability Registry and Perinatal Observatory.

Death: a metamorphosis for the spirit

Dictionary definition: Definitive loss by a living entity (organ, individual, tissue or cell) of the characteristic properties of life, leading to its destruction[10].

There is no factual evidence that I was in contact with a living being who had suffered death. The psychic told me so. It is only when the entity thanked me that we can deduce that the ghost state was suffered and unwanted, and the entity state was desired without being able to reach it alone. The thanks proved to me that the ghost was in an intermediate phase, a hybrid state, a state of unwanted wandering. The spirit was well in possession of all the information acquired during our cohabitation: the intervention of the medium changed the state of the ghost but not its content.

After death, the spirit regains its independence. It is no longer a prisoner of a biological envelope. The temporal constraint suffered through the earthly envelope disappears.

> « *Death is not the opposite of life.*
> *Life has no opposite.*
> *The opposite of death is birth.*
> *Life is eternal.* »
> Eckhart Tolle, The Power of Now, 2001

After sharing with the reader my experience in Niort, which lasted about a year and a half, some convictions are obvious to me. Thus, it seems obvious to me that death is only a change of

---

[10] Définitions issues du Dictionnaire en ligne Larousse.fr, Editions Larousse.

state for the spirit. This spirit during life makes full use of its bodily envelope: it allows it to exist in our earthly world in three dimensions, to be visible, to act and to interfere with matter and especially with other living beings. Once the physical envelope is worn out by time, it stops according to a slow process controlled by the spirit inhabiting it in the context of a natural death. Even before the body dies completely, the spirit has the power to detach itself from it to regain its state outside space-time. The spirit then regains its real dimension, its normal state. It lives past, present, and future. Its goal is then to join / find the other spheres.

In some cases, the spirit cannot completely detach itself from our material world. This is often the case in the case of a violent death, unwanted by the spirit that inhabits it. The spirit then enters a phase of wandering that can last for centuries on earth. It finds itself in an intermediate state, between our world and the first sphere, keeping certain human needs but finding it difficult to interact with matter. According to my experience in Niort, ghosts retain their entire state of consciousness. They are not in a vegetative state or in artificial survival. This energy then keeps the shape of its physical envelope but can pass through matter. It can be attached to a place without fully living this residue of earthly life. It wanders... not being part of any world. To me, it seems like the worst thing that can happen to us!

What does it need to reach his sphere? In my experience, it is still an energy that can allow it to do so by detaching himself from matter. The contact between a medium and a spirit determined to join its sphere allows it to find the resources it needs to reach the light tunnel serving as an interface between our world and the spheres. But these are special cases because, generally, the natural process allows the spirit to reach its sphere naturally.

Our bodies are composed of atoms like inert bodies. This means that inert matter can receive life. This body responds to physical laws. Its physical constitution is the same before and after death because atoms do not die. The difference comes from the fact that molecules are regularly identically replaced when we are alive but are not when we are dead. The difference is energetic. The mind provides the vital energy necessary to maintain order and coherence. Without a mind, the body moves towards disorder. Thus, we can say that spirit influences matter.

We can define death as a loss of the characteristic properties of life through the definitive and total decoupling of the spirit from its body envelope.

Proposed definition of death: definitive decoupling of spirit and body leading to its destruction.

The spirit: the vital energy of being

Dictionary definition: Intangible part of the human being, as opposed to the body, the matter[11]

Spirits represent the entities that have succeeded in reaching their sphere. From the last interaction I had with the spirit, I have evidence that a spirit can interfere with our dimension. I had also proof that a spirit knows our future. In addition, it came to thank me. So, it made the "effort" to come back and contact me. That means it was important to it. That is why I am convinced that it possessed emotions, respect and recognition. It seemed happy to have joined its sphere. I have no memory of any other form of ghost like the entities.

The mind is above all a quantity of energy. This quantity can vary to follow an earthly life. As things stand, it seems to me that these spirits remain attached to a sphere around our planet. Spirits may decide to return to earth this is the case of reincarnation. It is only after reaching a higher energy level that we will be able to reach higher spheres beyond our mother planet. Our state being primary, at the beginning of evolution, these spheres are currently inaccessible.

Spirits find themselves outside of time and space. They live past, present, and future at the same time. That is why the spirit justified its presence by saying that it was the last night that I would spend in this house: it had access to a view of my entire life and knew this situation.

---

[11] Definitions from the online dictionary Larousse.fr, Editions Larousse.

My experience shows that there can be interactions between us and spirits. There have always been beliefs through time, about spirits of light, celestial creatures, higher intelligences that help human beings and protect them from evil. These 'messengers', etymologically speaking, possess a considerable ability to help since the past and especially the future are all part of the same moment for them; that is why their advice is well-founded. Nevertheless, the person being helped retains the final decision since it is he or she who will choose the direction to take.

For what reason did the entity come to see me again in this house and not elsewhere? It could have thanked me the next day or a week later! What was the importance of this place? Because in the end, I have never seen this spirit ever since.

I suppose the spirit might have more eager coming back to this house rather than somewhere else. Or was it just to contain my anguish or my concerns? Indeed, I have never had a similar experience outside this house. I have never felt anxiety when I slept in a place I didn't know. But would it be the same if the spirit had come somewhere else, proving to me that it could reach me at any time? That would have been very anxiogenic in my opinion.

In literature, most approaches make a ternary distinction: body, soul, spirit. If we consider the soul as the headquarters of the activity shaping our individuality, of each proper being, it can be considered as a part of the mind serving as an interface between body and mind. It allows a harmonious relationship between the two because body and mind are not in opposition.

During its visit, the spirit had retained its own personality, its own soul.

I will therefore limit myself to Descartes' dualism: body and spirit that force us to ask ourselves what can unite them:

« There is a great difference between the spirit and the body, in that the body, of its nature, is always divisible, and the spirit is entirely indivisible. »
Descartes, Metaphysical Meditations

Spirit is not limited to our brain and it can influence matter. It remains connected to the entire universe. It is primarily made up of energy and seeks to increase its amount of energy.

« The motivation of the soul is its own increase»
Heraclitus, The Original Fragments - 5th c. BC

Thus, we can say that spirit is the second essential element in addition to matter to constitute a living being and to animate it.

Proposed definition of spirit: Vital source of a living being consisting of incorporated energy during an earthly life.

Earthly life and liberation of the spirit through biological evolution

Dictionary definition of life: Unique Characteristic to beings with complex structures (macromolecules, cells, organs, tissues), capable of resisting the various causes of change, able to renew, by assimilation, their constituent elements (atoms, small molecules), to grow and reproduce.

Dictionary definition of terrestrial life: Which takes place, which takes place on earth, as opposed to in heaven[12]

If we consider that the ghost always has a material structure, however tiny it may be, the first part of the definition remains true. It seems to me to be consistent with my observations if one adds a little bit of energy. If by autonomous activity we mean the ability to believe and to move where it wants, this point is also consistent with my observations.

However, this autonomy seems to be limited to these elements like a prisoner in his cell with no possibility of interacting with other beings.

We could imagine that earthly life is the time that elapses between life and death. But my experience shows me a different approach. This experience shows that it is the spirit that defines the end on earth and certainly the beginning. I deduce that the end of the earthly life takes place when the spirit reaches the first sphere and not when the spirit leaves its fleshly envelope.

Earthly life is above all the life we know: birth, acquisition of knowledge and autonomy, then death. To be more precise, earthly life begins when the spirit integrates the earthly envelope

---

[12] Definitions from the online dictionary Larousse.fr, Editions Larousse.

and ends when the spirit joins the first sphere. Nowadays, death is observed according to the physical envelope but not to the spirit.

What about birth and intrauterine life of the baby? I would tend to say that since science has shown that the acquisition of knowledge begins before birth, the mind integrates the body long before birth. If we take the example of in vitro fertilization (IVF), I am convinced of the constitution of the body-mind pair at the time of IVF. The appropriation of this new body can only be progressive and reach its paroxysm at the time of the first heartbeats, sign of the beginning of autonomy. Thus, the poet Khalil Gibran tells us in The Prophet: "Your children are not your children but the sons and daughters of the call of Life to itself, they come through you but not from you, and although they are with you, they do not belong to you...". Finally, the first breath of air marks the final stage of incarnation.

This scenario of an incarnation of a spirit in a body implies the consideration of a fully adult being from the start and must be considered as such. Its destiny is already established.

For dualists, matter and spirit are two realities that exist independently from one another, but whose union allows the appearance of a sensitive or intelligent life. Each human is made up of a body and a spirit that interact closely. It is this spirit that provides its individuality and uniqueness on each human being. Moreover, it has the power to transgress material laws through miracles or paranormal phenomena. The spirit, therefore the individual, survives the death of the physical organism. This conception is very widespread in the East.

For what reasons could this phenomenon not happen again?

I am inclined to believe in the possibility of reincarnation of a spirit. Only the earthly life allows the spirit to evolve from one sphere to another, only the earthly life allows the spirit to evolve at the energetic level. And it is only at the time of the earthly lives that the spirit can interact, thus reach new higher energy levels, new higher spheres.

What is the difference between Life and life?

During our earthly life we have a physical existence, we possess an envelope built from earthly elements, palpable to be adapted to life on earth. There is no doubt, the best place where we can live with this body envelope is the Earth. This is the current result of this slow process called "evolution".

How can we understand biological evolution?

When we talk about evolution, we are talking about the evolution of our body envelope and the changes we can see over time that allow the best possible adaptation to our planet Earth. It allows us, above all, to mainly adapt ourselves to the atmospheric pressure, the length of a day, the length of the seasons, the dependencies to the stars like the sun, notably the variation of ambient temperature, or the moon with its gravitational impacts. For this, nothing can replace time because evolution is comparable to a long chain in which we represent a simple link. Any transmission from one link to another considers its experience.

Until now, the law of the strongest could be decisive. The physically strongest must certainly be the one best suited to his local environment. Having said that, the determining element is not to be adapted to a single local area, the mobility of groups has allowed the construction of a first network, the first interactions, the first exchanges, the first sharing and the first riches that make us Men. Adaptation can only occur in relation with the planet, otherwise any change in parameter can lead to eradication.

Trade has allowed ideas to disseminate, to develop trust and cooperation, to maintain peace most of the time. But it has also facilitated the spread of disease.

Homo Sapiens has become the species that has preponderance over other species by influence, number, and extent. It is the dominant species on planet Earth.

But while our power is unquestionable, our success is collective, not individual. It is based on numerous genetic intermingling. The history of mankind is bushy! I like this approach very much because it is the only non-dogmatic scientific approach that allows us to permanently question what we think we know.

Other living beings are capable of cooperating in large numbers: mammals for the most part but not only. Ants and bees are good examples. It is not surprising that we are now talking about trees or other living beings considered less evolved...

Our specificity is the flexibility of our established systems of social cooperation. Adaptation once again. But this time we are reaching the stage of being able to adapt our environment to ourselves and not the other way round. We live in places with a constant temperature, we light up whenever we want and bring drinking water wherever we want.

And it goes even further! We are in the process of building an "ambient intelligence" environment where all the elements that create it will soon possess some intelligence as well. This way we will be able to accelerate our own evolution. This ambient intelligence will shift the boundaries of our own intelligence. Thus, a being considered intelligent today may not be intelligent in a hundred years' time! Our envelope will have to evolve to adapt to this new environment.

To follow these millions of years of existence, we are managing to take our evolution in hand at the cost of a real ethnic cleansing with the suppression of many species. Natural selection is being replaced by intelligently organised selection. These disappearances have not all been caused by Man, but his evolution has often benefited from them. This is the case of mammoths, woolly rhinoceroses, and cave bears, whom did not survive the disappearance of their biotope at the end of the last ice age, thus reducing the number of threats to Humans.

Time allows us to shape our environment, our body envelopes and thus facilitate our interactions. But this very time imposes on us a beginning and an end of earthly life since it is necessary to be in possession of an interface to interact. The interface used is our body which allows us to touch, carry, manufacture, shape, destroy, sculpt our environment. Human evolution tends towards a body construction to facilitate the expression of the spirit. Our evolution will be complete when our body will no longer have any constraints to allow our mind to express itself while using our body shaped as we wish to interact continuously. Thus, our mind will be able to interact freely and without constraint on living matter and its environment.

The evolution of our earthly body is done with the following steps:
- Search for the best adaptation to the earth's environment and autonomy,

- Always looking for the best adaptation with a clearance of space,
- Always looking for the best adaptation with a clearance of space and a clearance of time.

Today's world is entering the era of communication, with fibre optics and the Internet promoting virtual contact for an ever-increasing number of people. Geographical location no longer matters, soon the language used will no longer matter. I would therefore tend to say that we are entering the second phase of evolution: the clearance of space.

We can also notice that the "I have" is gradually being replaced by the "I am" in our leading societies. Possession loses its importance in order to give priority to the present time, to lived actions, to the sharing of events that can be associated with a communion. Thus, the amount of the salary loses its importance in the face of the possibility of going on holiday, births are events where one wishes to be present, welcoming the baby in the place of life a shared moment. Even the football world championship is felt to be shared by all at the same time. For most of us, this experience goes far beyond knowing the winner because in the end there is no stake for the spectator. The pleasure comes above all from this spiritual union with millions of people who share the players' conditions and the feeling of being all together at the same time. This need to commune is a way of interacting.

Evolution is not synonymous with local adaptation, otherwise it could have catastrophic consequences. You only have to look at the number of animals that are disappearing as a result of global warming to understand this. Darwin's theory describes an end-of-evolution process for species that are, for one reason or another, cut off from other living things in other environments. Island life is a good example. With insufficient genetic renewal, dominant beings take over and steer genetic evolution towards a dead end: the local specialization of the earth's body.

Man is adapted to life on earth without further local specialisation. He can live near the poles as well as near the equator, on the seashore as well as at high altitudes. Evolution gives priority to the expression of the spirit and not to adaptation to the local environment, hence a simple skeletal structure for Man giving priority to autonomy, interaction and contact. The five senses exist and are used by Man without being very efficient. And yet, we dominate other living beings because we are in possession of a body envelope allowing the spirit to express itself more easily.

Imagine being a tree and trying to interact with your environment ... with the same level of intelligence, the ability to know, to understand, it would be difficult for you to share it! Imagine you are a monkey... with the same level of intelligence, it would be impossible for you to express yourself completely: your jaw does not allow you to articulate, your hands do not allow you to do fine manual work, your legs do not allow you to move easily. Despite limited cognitive, expressive and adaptive performances, I remain convinced that intelligence is not a characteristic of man, whatever some scientists may think.

When we talk about intelligence in our societies, we usually talk about our power to express what we think or know. In this case, it seems obvious that Man possesses the most evolved body envelope. This does not mean that other living beings do not possess a similar level of intelligence. And yet, our spirit, cramped in our body, is still not able to express itself completely. Reducing and then eliminating these interface constraints between our mind and our physical world corresponds to the finality of the evolution of living beings. Our evolution has only just begun ...

What are the key factors of evolution at the human level?

The purpose of a living being is to develop the ability to stay connected with other energies. Moreover, evolution has always rewarded cooperative strategies.
The main levels are as follows:
- Mutualization and networking,
- Fusion allowing the emergence of a global intelligence,
- Absorption to the universal system.

What is the role of technologies?

Their role is particularly important in evolution. Indeed, they allow us to push back the natural limits and to progressively take control of it to orient it according to our wishes. It is still necessary to know the purpose of our evolution, namely the liberation of the mind, otherwise there is a danger of going in the wrong direction.

We talk a lot about the advantages of technology but little about the disadvantages. One point I think is important to bear in mind: any new stage does not or very rarely replace the previous ones but adds an extra layer. Let us give a concrete example by talking about the book. The arrival of digital technology has not suppressed paper books but seeks to save it for luxury editions. It is the same for music where vinyl should have disappeared with the digital but this was not the case.

We must expect an increasingly complex world in which different levels of technology coexist, from the simplest to the most complex. The world's population is becoming more and more fragmented, split up because of the emergence of new technologies, and this is only just beginning! A part of the population will not be able to benefit from the new technologies because of financial, cognitive, or educational problems. These growing gaps can only generate growing tensions and global instability. *From the growth of technology emerges the social gap, a source of global discord.*

Russian cosmism is an interesting approach if one limits oneself to the vision of the world which is based on the idea of the indissoluble unity of Man and the cosmos, of the spiritual relationship between the inner and outer world.

« *Man is similar to the Cosmos, but not because he is a tiny part of it. It is because he is in himself a whole Cosmos, and his composition resembles that of the Cosmos.* », This is the definition given by Nikolai Berdiaev, one of the most famous Russian philosophers of the early 20th century.

Some scientists believe that the evolution of our envelope is moving towards genetic degeneration. But this will not be the end of the evolution of Man if he takes charge of his own evolution, if he directs his evolution as he wishes, i.e. by allowing the spirit to express itself without constraint. We observe the beginnings of the theories of "augmented man" which are currently moving in this direction. To go further. To go even further...

Overall, if we consider the strong dependence between life and energy, between energy and the universe, there is no life without a universe and vice versa. *Life exists throughout the universe.* Human evolution as taught in Europe will have to be rewritten one day because it does not consider the interplay with extra-terrestrial life. As earthly life is part of a whole, we must review its origin, its evolution and the purpose of its current teaching.

Proposed Definition of Life: A point energy phenomenon that allows organisms to interact.

Proposed definition of terrestrial life: Energy point phenomena that allow organisms to interact on or from the Earth.

Interacting: the way to use our free will

Dictionary definition: To have with something else a reciprocal action[13]

Throughout the period I lived, the ghost came to see me out of necessity: it wanted to take energy from me. The consequence for me was to be tired all the time and this loss really appeared as a lack for my organism.
My story shows that the intervention of the medium allowed the entity to leave the place, to leave our dimension. It is indeed the contact with the medium that allowed the ghost this complete change of state. It never asked for help on this point, it never tried to communicate with me before the intervention of the medium, which it accepted and was grateful for the result.

But what is this force that allows the medium to give sufficient energy to a ghost to reach the expected sphere? Interacting does not only mean "being in contact", "shaking hands" or "acting together". In our case, interacting means establishing an energy flow between two entities, one considered dead and the other considered alive.

In describing the importance of earthly interrelationships, the relationship between medium and entity is quite restrictive because they are the basis of everything. The contact between living beings is especially important. If an entity can change or make material dependencies disappear, and thus change dimension, we can imagine that our contacts can also make our dependencies evolve. A contact seems little and yet the impact

---

[13] Definitions from the online dictionary Larousse.fr, Editions Larousse.

for the entity seems to have been decisive and unlimited in time: the state of the ghost has been transformed.

The contact is not exclusively physical: a thought, an intention can carry a lot of weight. Some can have the same weight as an action, or even more! In our case, these inter-actuations have a link with time. Any inter-acting creates inertia and it is perhaps also a way to slow down time or to extract oneself temporarily from it.

Interaction is indeed the main way to evolve during our earthly life. We made the choice to be on earth to interact yes, it is indeed us who chose to come on earth, so we transform our environment and we change the concepts of the people we are with. We therefore necessarily leave a trace of what we have done or said intentionally.

«The encounter between two personalities is like the contact of two chemical substances; if there is a reaction, both are transformed. »
Carl Gustav Jung, Swiss psychiatric doctor

Whatever happens, we enjoy our free will, we resonate. As much as interactions are information, the contrary is not necessarily true. The mistake is to reason in the present without considering the leverage effect on the future. Our interactions do not only have an impact on the consequences that we can see, but on all future impacts.

I could give an Old Testament example: Cain and Abel. Cain, banished by God for murdering his brother, becomes cursed on earth. He becomes a wanderer and a vagabond. It is said: « *From God's point of view, an assassination is not limited to the death of a single being, but to all his descendants.* »

Our actions continually change the future. This leverage effect is decisive in identifying the actions to be taken during our earthly life. To make an impression, we can say that our actions have an impact on the entire universe. Each of us has a responsibility for the future of all of us and for our personal future; one day or another, we ourselves will be confronted with the future we have shaped.

Proposed definition of interacting: To establish a lasting reciprocal link with something else.

Conscience: our collective steering system

Dictionary definition: knowledge, intuitive or immediate reflexive, that everyone has of their own existence and that of the outside world.[14].

When the spirit was thanking me, it appeared to me that it was in full possession of the consciousness of the ghost with whom I had cohabited. There is therefore continuity of consciousness between the state of the ghost and the state of mind.

My experience makes me say that the ghost is well linked to our space-time contrary to the spirit. Otherwise, why would it have changed its behaviour between the first days when it exercised violence against me and the following days when it limited itself to taking the energy it needed? The ghost did not know our future while the spirit did.

I make a distinction between the notion of mind and the notion of consciousness. Consciousness is used as a well of data allowing, thanks to its intelligence, to bring up useful information and to "process" it. During our earthly life, consciousness allows us to analyse, adapt and decide, it seems to me, through the filter constituted by our brain or our body in a more general way. It proposes the direction to take without imposing it on us, because we keep our free will. We thus understand why our past lives do not naturally go back to our brain because it is not a priority in comparison with our experience acquired during our present life. Moreover, we can imagine that this "reset" at the moment of our arrival on earth

---

[14] Definitions from the online dictionary Larousse.fr, Editions Larousse.

facilitates an assessment of the events lived during the last life, at the moment of our earthly death.

The spirit is mainly attached to the consciousness, it is now for me a certainty. The ghost I was dealing with, thought, knew what he was doing and had immediate knowledge of the situation. Consciousness survives death, exists beyond time and space, beyond our space-time. In my story, the ghost knows that it is in an unsuitable place and knows the circumstances of its death in its last earthly life. It accepts the medium's contact, accepts his help in the hope of a better condition. Its thanks indicate that it feels better after his intervention. It makes the link between my presence in this house, the medium's intervention, and its change of state.

In systemic domain, every system has three levels:
- The operating system, which allows you to transform input elements into output elements,
- The information system for acquiring, storing, processing and disseminating information,
- The mission of the steering system is to steer the overall system towards the objectives set for it, and to verify that these objectives have been achieved.

As much as consciousness can contain the information system and the steering system the spirit has proven to contain both levels during our contact as much, I did not find a system operating at my level which is usually the most obvious part of a system. Yet every system has one. But still, one must know the purpose of consciousness to identify the process of transformation through it. I think that matter is a crystallization of consciousness and it is not the brain that creates consciousness.

But what is consciousness really?

At the beginning of my reflections, I imagined consciousness as a beach of fine sand. When a being decides to travel on earth, he takes a handful of sand with him. When we return, the handful, enriched by our experience, is returned to this beach. During reincarnation, the handful remains globally the same with always some deviations that can explain the differences in personalities and past experiences. These two concepts, the beach and the handful of sand correspond to the collective consciousness and the individual consciousness. During my reflections, it appears that this consciousness is out of space-time: whatever the original place of this handful of sand, it will always remain connected with its beach.

We can imagine that everything is conscious. Individual consciousness can only partially express itself through the body. Only a part of this consciousness emerges with a certain autonomy that it needs. Our brain will know how to partially bring back to its conscious surface information it needs as well as intentions present in its subconscious.

The individual consciousness remains nested in the collective consciousness while respecting the free will of the being. Positioning this collective consciousness at the level of the earth seems coherent to me. We can imagine other higher levels encompassing this first one before arriving at the last level: cosmic consciousness.

The spirit came to thank me but not the medium or I didn't know about it, why? Maybe it did it in its own way, I don't know. In any case, the medium would not have come to the house if I had not lived in that house all that time, if I had not discussed these phenomena with Elise and if I had not stayed that day of

November 11th in Niort. I hesitated for a long time to stay there alone on that holiday. But the decision to rest alone carried more weight than a trip to Marseille or Paris to enjoy moments with friends. It seems rather inconsistent in retrospect, but this decision finally changed my life. It shows once again that a decision, which may seem insignificant at first sight, can put you on the right path.

To understand the impacts of our interactions, we need to visualize them outside of time: this is an extraordinary leverage effect. A person who crushes an ant on his way does not only kill that ant but all its offspring. A person who kills another person stops his interactions for this earthly life and can generate impacts on his descendants.

I do not dissociate the consciousness from the freedom that allows us to live in the first person. Consciousness is not individualistic. It allows us to distinguish good from evil, it helps us to find our path adapted to our destiny since it represents a field of possibilities.

Proposed definition of consciousness: immaterial and timeless system of control, information, and operation, inseparable from the spirit.

Religion: a set of values adapted to our societies

Dictionary definition: A specific set of beliefs and dogmas defining the relationship between human beings and the sacred[15]

This experience shows me the existence of a continuation after earthly death as most religions affirm. Death, if it normally puts an end to earthly life, is not the ultimate end of man's destiny. The entity informs me of the existence of a state of bliss thanks to the intervention of the medium. This is indeed the first common point to most religions. This state did appear following the state of confinement in which it was found.

However, this experience does not directly provide information on a logic of merit or morality of retribution beyond death. This depends closely on the actions carried out during earthly life. Yet this is the second common point to most religions. Nevertheless, the last contact with the entity allows us to find differences between ghost state and entity state. As much as the daily visits did not allow any communication between us, the interaction being limited to a "robbery" of energy, this last contact brought respect, real recognition and even love. The entity's return to normal brought it, without a doubt, this state of rapture that it wished to share.

The first Men focused on the cult of the dead, fertility, and nature, which are the origins of beliefs and rites. There were multiple cults, different in their expression but similar in their aspirations. Through these rites, the following fundamental questions were already being asked:

---

[15] Definitions from the online dictionary Larousse.fr, Editions Larousse.

- Where am I going (after death)?
- Where do I come from (before birth)?
- Who am I (as a living being)?

These questions were all the stronger as the life span was short and the ephemeral passage on earth obvious.

The funerary rites of megalithic civilizations show rigorous rites leaving nothing to chance collective or individual burial, placement of human remains or body, joint offerings. All this staging is not only aimed at bringing the dead to life in the memory of the living, for it is the events that took place beforehand that take precedence. This care also demonstrates the will to accompany the deceased beyond his death as if the existence of an immortal spirit was already manifest ...

These behaviours are not necessarily linked to a religious structure. They are only considered as cults, not necessarily linked to a deity. All it needs is for a group of people to consider structuring to organize rituals or to share beliefs. The notion of "sacred" is not linked to a religious cult either.

Religions bring an adaptation of universal rules for our earthly life. Thus, we find there a common core: existence of the notion of God, doing good and not evil, and feeling earthly life as suffering.

Our world today cannot exist without religions. We do not have sufficient scientific knowledge to justify what they impose through dogmas that are often rightly but not factually based. They answer questions about the human condition to bring social cohesion.

These are God's advices/requirements! Who could be against it? These religions, often adapted to local specificities linked to the climate and the organization of society, are structuring and bring daily well-being to all. They allow and facilitate a life in society and provide answers to questions without going through science. It is an obligatory "tutor" for primitive people such as ours who seek to evolve and live serenely.

It is a world in perpetual proliferation: 124,000 prophets are recognized from the different monotheistic traditions! And each religion relies on a few texts judiciously selected from the many apocryphal sources. Whether these religions are the fruit of human reflection or of messages provided by supreme beings, they are essential. They give positive directions, provided they are well interpreted, and they allow men to live together in good conditions, thus initiating a global coherence. Their structures are more or less complex as well as their hierarchizations.

Everything that is structured is structuring!

There are four fundamental elements common to all religious beliefs [16] :
1) The existence of a world beyond,
2) The presence of a cult,
3) The presence of rules and values intended to regulate daily life,
4) The presence of specialists who provide the link between our earthly world and the afterlife.

---

[16] Article by Jean-François Dortier in Sciences Humaines of February 2017.

Above all, religion serves less to face death than to face the trials of earthly life. It allows us to connect people to one another by founding communities of belonging.

Proposed definition of religion: A specific set of beliefs and dogmas proposed by an organization in order to pre-establish rules and values essential to life in society.

Time: a notion linked to the matter imagined by humans

Dictionary definition: A fundamental concept conceived as an infinite medium in which events follow one another[17].

My experience has shown me a great difference between the ghost and the spirit. The ghost is attached to place, so it is not detached from our time, whereas the spirit is totally detached from our world. Past, present, and future had no distinction for the spirit at the time of its thanks. He said that the night in this house was its last. Perhaps it was a wink from it knowing full well the impact on my life that it would have? Beyond that last night, did it know of the existence of this book and the awareness that it would bring?

« *What is time?*
If no one asks me, I know;
if I want to answer, I don't know. »
Saint Augustine, The Confessions, Book XI

What a beautiful paradox! We possess this notion of time within ourselves as a matter of course. But when we must conceptualize it, it puts us at a disadvantage! The characteristic of life is to contain two completely distinct elements, dependent on different dimensions: body and mind. A part of us escapes time. I remain convinced that our earthly life is a particular, extremely specific case that offers us an opening to the mastery of our future. It is only during these punctual moments that we can interact on matter, interact with other living beings to help each other to rise. Our point of reference will remain earth, our mother planet, and

---

[17] Definitions from the online dictionary Larousse.fr, Editions Larousse

terrestrial life will remain a cycle. Our clock describes only a duration, duration from the moment we set it in motion. One day is the amount of time our planet needs to spin. One year is the amount of time our planet needs to spin around the sun. But who can say that the time of one day is the same as that of another? For a living being, depending on its interactions, its dimension is quite suggestive according to its experience. We all feel the relativity of time.

Marcel Proust said: « *Days may be equal for a clock, but not for a man.* ». What a wonderful truth!

When there is a break in a state, a change, a movement, we perceive time because it is affected. When this same event takes place in a cyclic phenomenon, it is not a repetition, it is the participation in a single event. This is how our rituals or ceremonies allow us to extract ourselves from this continuum. Since time is ultimately based on repetitive cycles, I believe that time does not exist.

« *Does the future already exist in advance?*[18] »

We can predict the impact of a bullet launch, we can calculate the trajectory of a rocket. We can, with the elements in our possession at a given moment, anticipate the impacts of an event in the near future. We then follow the lines of the universe with a unidirectional time arrow. But this is only an illusion because our space-time remains dynamic. There are several futures that can become real, hence the existence of our free will.

---

[18] Etienne Klein, "Does the future already exist in the future? "Editions du Temps, N°1, March 2014.

« Time and space are not conditions of existence, time and space are a model for reflection. »
Albert Einstein

Proposed definition of time: fundamental notion designed to determine durations with the movement of our planet and the stars as a reference.

Energy: a fundamental principle

Dictionary definition: Someone's physical power, allowing one to act, and react.[19]

This definition sounds like a misnomer because power is energy produced or consumed per unit of time. In this book, we talk about vital energy which does not seem to be taken into account in the dictionary. Yet this notion exists in Chinese or Japanese medicine.

Over the months, the ghost had a regular need for energy. This vital energy was "stolen" from me at chest level, starting from my neck. The ghost was able to pump it out with an invisible spike. Was it its teeth, as in the vampire tradition? I don't really know, in those moments my head was wrapped by the entity, so I couldn't see it anymore.

When I asked the medium if the ghost had given me back my energy, she answered that she had already asked. This indicates that the medium had thought about it as if it was something important, as if this "robbery" could have an impact on me. Without even knowing anything about it, it seemed important to me. I can well imagine, in this case, a collapse of the immune system that would result in illness.

Its need to supplement energy on a regular basis shows that a ghost is not an "isolated system"[20], otherwise it would conserve

---

[19] Definitions from the online dictionary Larousse.fr, Editions Larousse

[20] Thermodynamics offers three types of systems: "closed system" without exchange of matter but with exchange of energy, "isolated system" without exchange of matter and energy, "open system" with exchange of matter and energy.

its total energy (it is the first thermodynamic law that specifies it) and could not exchange energy with the outside.

The existence of ghosts would run counter to the second law of thermodynamics. Recall that this law requires that the total entropy of an isolated system increases inexorably over time. Thus, the energy usable by the system is lost as time passes and disorder sets in. And, without external energy, it is impossible to reverse the bar.

« *If we cannot touch or interact with ghosts, it is because they are necessarily made of energy and not matter. However, if the second law of thermodynamics is true, energy is lost and it would be impossible for such entities to maintain their existence for a significant period of time.* », concludes Brian Cox[21], British physicist.

That said, the Niort experiment shows that not only are ghosts very well defined in space when I passed my hand, the "boundary" between space and ghost was delimited by a much colder temperature change within its volume; it would even have been possible to calculate its volume or temperature, but also, they have the ability to "steal" energy. Thus, they fill up with energy, regularly, to maintain a certain level or increase it, so there is a variation of entropy within them. This would mean that a ghost, like a living being, is an open system in the thermodynamic sense of the term: there are exchanges between the system and the outside, even tiny ones! The living being exchanges matter to make energy. This is indeed the case when we feed ourselves: the various chemical reactions allow our metabolism to function. The ghost, unable to transform matter

---

[21] https://www.futura-sciences.com/sciences/questions-reponses/physique-fantomes-nexistent-pas-explications-scientifiques-7578/

into energy itself, is forced to find already existing sources of energy to "fill up". It used me as a tank of energy without worrying about the consequences that it might have on me.

Is it a question of the ghost's survival ? or an attempt to reach its sphere?
Can a ghost that lacks energy "die" a second time?

Even though the thermostat turned on when the ghost passed by, I did not feel there was any significant "exchange" of heat between the environment and its cold space. There seemed to be some kind of insulating blanket around this ghost. It should be pointed out that there was very little space between the bed and the wall when the ghost passed by, so the convector was enclosed in its volume as it passed.

On the one hand, it appears that the molecules forming it seem less agitated, hence the cold accompanying it, on the other hand, the light halo, however weak it may be, shows its loss of energy, if we take into account quantum physics.

The universe is all about energy. Absolute vacuum does not exist, energy is everywhere in variable quantities. There can be no living being without energy.

The history of Niort refers to small amounts of energy which have nevertheless had consequences on a human being. If we add up the energy consumed by all living beings on earth, this quantity is not negligible for us, but it is for the universe. If we cumulate the energies of the living beings making up the universe, would this volume become large enough to impact the future of the universe? Can we imagine that living beings could thus control the universe? This is a line of thought that should not be neglected.

As far as the ghost's actions are concerned, I do not think it meant me any harm because it knew from the beginning the outcome of this story and the fact that it would be able to free itself from the situation. We were linked for a short time with a loan of energy, necessary to achieve the desired result. A win-win story! It allowed the ghost to get out of the situation and me to become aware of the reality of earthly life and the relativity of time.

In any case, Life is energy and energy never dies, it is transformed. The phenomenon of incarnation at the moment of birth remains unexplained. But it seems absurd to me to imagine that this event can happen only once in eternity. Reincarnation is therefore the most plausible scenario. I believe in possible reincarnations as the levels of energy accumulated, as the envelope evolves.

« *I believe in an afterlife,*
Simply because energy cannot die;
It flows, it transforms, and it never stops. »
Albert Einstein

Proposed definition of energy: a fundamental and inseparable principle of the universe and life.

God: the cosmic consciousness

Dictionary definition: To be eternal, unique, and creative. Superior being endowed with supernatural power[22].

Religions affirm the existence of one or more Gods. It may have a different name: Supreme Being, Eternal, Allah, Alpha and Omega, Creator, Great Being, Great Architect, Jahweh, Jehovah, Lord, Almighty, Divinity, Logos, Father, Providence, Savior, Trinity, Word... It is always the same concept with some variations according to places and times.

The evolution in the Egyptian religion seems interesting to me. From the third royal dynasty onwards, a gentle reform of theology pushed the Egyptians to adore one God, first with obedience and without resistance, then with democratization and survival after death. This monotheist, rather than polytheist, shows, in my opinion, a certain theological maturity.

Following my experience in Niort, it appears to me that God represents the totality of the energies that make up our minds. The energy composing the spirit comes from a more important source and is inseparable from this source, like a magnet, it remains attracted by its source. This universal energy mass allows certain elements to escape in certain cases to allow life to exist. *God is a whole, we compose God as God is within us.* Life is nothing without God and God has no reason to exist without Life. God exists because of the universe as the universe exists because of God.

---

[22] Definitions from the online dictionary Larousse.fr, Editions Larousse

It seems to me, therefore, that God is not transcendent and no more immanent towards Man. Not only does God belong to a higher order without being outside the world we know, but God is not on the same level as Man.

We can make a link with the notion of collective consciousness outside our four-dimensional space-time. If we imagine that the purpose of this consciousness is to increase the entropy of the universe, we can imagine that its operating system is made up of living beings whose destiny is the optimization of their energy level. This being shared at the moment of the liberation of the spirit, at the moment of death, with this collective consciousness.

Does the notion of creation of the universe finally have a meaning? It does not appear to me that God is in the role of creator but rather that he is an indispensable element of the universe to build and organize it. He therefore appears to have a role as an architect.

There is only one God.

We find ourselves in a timeless situation that is difficult to conceive with our earthly logics.

> « *God is an infinite sphere, whose centre is everywhere and whose circumference is nowhere.* »
> Blaise Pascal, Les pensées, 1670

Proposed definition of God: The eternal, unique and foundational set of energies enabling the existence of the universe and Life.

Third part

The destiny

« It's not just where you go that gives life meaning, but also the way you get there »

Marc Levy, Vous revoir, 2005

The purpose of this third part is to describe my theory about destiny during earthly life. By "theory" I mean an "*organized set of scientific principles, rules, and laws designed to describe and explain a set of facts.* ».

When we consult the dictionary, we find the following definition for the term "destiny": "*A pre-established determination of the events of human life by a higher power.*[23]».

So we learn that destiny is only pre-established for the human being. Why is that? Aren't other living beings affected by a destiny? What is it that separates us from other living beings in this area? It is determined (it is said) by a "higher power". But which one? We will come back to this later.

The first question one must ask is "What makes sense to me in general? »

To this end, it is advisable to develop:
— The *feeling* of having an influence on our immediate environment;
— The *realization* of one's personal potential;
— *Belonging* to at least one, if not two or three communities.

But unfortunately, that is not enough. Giving meaning to one's life does not necessarily determine one's destiny, but it does play a major part in it because it facilitates interaction. When we find

---

[23] Definitions from the online dictionary Larousse.fr, Editions Larousse.

meaning in our actions, we become more optimistic, more socially inserted. It is an essential condition to go further.

We must then be convinced to bring meaning to a whole of which we are a part. Somewhere, it is necessary to find the right frequency to be able to resonate with this whole.
For this, it is necessary to be able to evaluate the energy level from which we start in order to be able to acquire even more energy. Destiny can be linked to the actions to be carried out to be able to raise our energy level from the level from which we start at the beginning of each earthly life. That is why our destiny is personal.

The higher our spirit is energetically, the more we use a complex body envelope. As a human being, we use the envelope resulting from the current earthly evolution: our 10^{14} living cells which compose us as well as our 10^{26} atoms!

We all seek to develop this spirit from what we have learned from previous lives. We can consider this achievement as our own even if it also feeds the achievement of all living beings on Earth since we are a unity of this whole, just as the spirit feeds the achievement of our universal grouping since it constitutes a unity of this whole.

We remain masters of all the slow processes that govern us, we are therefore masters of our earthly life. Is not earthly life a complex set of slow processes over a limited period of time? This is how we can decide to be born when we feel the need and even to die when we feel the time comes. These elements can be disrupted by unexpected events that generate violent deaths such as illness or accident, for which our decision is conditioned. This is not an aporetic reasoning: it is in these circumstances that the process can be disrupted and make us live an intermediate, hybrid, unwanted period and thus... become ghosts.

Over time, human evolution allows us to limit unintended impacts to allow the spirit to express itself more simply and sustainably. Exercising free will. Thus, technologies and evolution of our earthly envelope, will allow us to reach the extreme level where the spirit will no longer need the body as an interface to interact with matter.

During our earthly life, we undergo the impacts of gravitation and time so our physical envelope is essential for us to be able to exist and interact within our world. Outside this renewable earthly period, time does not exist. My experience in Niort has shown me that there are sometimes problems, during the change of state, which keep the spirit, then ghostly, between two. The spirit remains too adherent to matter preventing it from reaching another dimension. Whatever the energy of a ghost, its lack of atoms does not allow it to interact easily with objects or living beings but it allows it to cross any matter. Only an external help allows it to free itself from the little remaining matter to become again an energy system independent of our space-time.

We are entering the era of communication and the removal of space constraint. This virtual, and soon permanent, interconnection makes us aware of this increasingly powerful, increasingly effective collective intelligence. We are also beginning to receive a global view of our effects, both on ourselves and on our mother planet.

When I hear Mae Jemison, the first African American woman to travel in space, say, "The future is not a matter of luck, it's being built". When I read Will Durant and his wife Ariel, American writers and philosophers, saying, "the future never just happened, it was created," it gives me real hope for believing in the potential of humanity, the leader of the world living on Earth, for becoming aware of the essential things and our responsibilities, and for serenely fulfilling our destiny. Everything we do must be seen with the leverage of time; the balance being taken over the whole of space - time. Thus, the being who saves one life, saves all future generations, the being who takes one life, destroys all future generations. Beyond these extremes, we shape the future through all our interactions and their consequences. Reality is built out of time. It is in this way, through detachment from our earthly life, our space and our time, that the personal assessment is made. Christianity calls this stage the special judgment. This judgment brings to light a man's unique life, his freedom and personal responsibility and decides his eternal destiny (Catechism of the Catholic Church n.1022).

We have all agreed to return to earth in possession of our individual consciousness. We all have a role to play in building our future and that of future generations. We have all accepted a mission. This destiny is within us. The direction is given to us, we still have to find the best path to reach our goals in our lives. Trust yourself, listen to yourself, *"know yourself[24]"* and find happiness because the right direction you find brings you happiness and more. I'm not talking about selfish happiness which is not one, I'm talking about happiness shared with others because happiness is linked to interaction.

It is this well-being that teenagers discover when they are together, they do not need to talk, they are together and feel good. It is this well-being that we feel when we make love, when two bodies merge but also two minds over a period of time that seems impossible to evaluate. It is this well-being that appears when we

---

[24] Motto inscribed on the frontispiece of the Temple of Delphi that Socrates took over according to la-philosophie.com

feel empathy with another person and when we instinctively understand their feelings without experiencing them. These are the moments when one feels radiated with positive impacts around oneself, when one enters in resonance with others, when one makes other beings happy. These are all attempts, sometimes successful, to resonate. We experience the immediacy and the measure of the feeling of the situation and this remains specific to the people living it. My conviction is that we have the possibility to permanently correlate our consciences. This situation is comparable to the "entangled state[25]" of quantum mechanics where the states remain dependent on each other, no matter how far apart they may be.

To be a good listener, all the difficulty is to find a balance between the needs of our envelope (our body) made up of atoms provided by our mother earth - and our mind outside our space and time. Life makes the link between two different worlds governed by different laws. One, a material world, benefits from the present time to be able to shape the future and the other, the spirit, purely energetic, is the result of earthly actions without being located in our space - time. What a paradox! Some scientists would say that life exists to combat the entropy of the ever-expanding universe. Perhaps this is the finality of our destinies? Are we the policemen of the universe?

Our modern societies are blinding us, so let us be vigilant and not lose sight of our fundamentals. They force us to compete and seek performance. All this goes against spirituality and true

---

[25] The entanglement principle states that two particles that have interacted at some point in their existence can form an entangled system forever, even when the particles are separated.
https://www.sciencesetavenir.fr/fondamental/premiere-photo-d-une-intrication-quantique_136308

values, namely, finding peace, serenity and participating in the whole. Let's not forget either that we are at the very beginning of an evolution. We do not yet understand much... Let us stay humble...

« *Whoever pretends to set himself up as Judge of truth and knowledge exposes himself to perish under the laughter of the gods since we do not know how things really are and we only know the representation we make of them* ». Albert Einstein Alert.

Let us not forget that we retain our free will no matter what happens while remaining connected with the other living beings with whom we interact. This phenomenon is similar to the vibratory phenomenon that allows us to enter into resonance. It is from a return on oneself that each one ends up finding the meaning of his life, which brings the joy of having found oneself again. "*You don't exist to impress the world. You exist to live your life in a way that will make you happy*" says Richard Bach, an American writer.

Earthly life is an individual experience: we own our carnal envelope, it serves as an interface with the rest of the world, it allows us to express ourselves, communicate and create links with other spirits. And this does not contradict the fact that we seek to interact throughout our lives and participate in the construction of a collective future.

Determinism or free will?

Philosophers such as Spinoza or Descartes ask us to choose one or the other while both cohabit: our body envelope undergoes the laws of classical physics while benefiting from a free will proper to living beings thanks to our mind. Henri Poincaré, French mathematician, physicist, philosopher, and engineer, said: *"Chance is only the measure of our ignorance*[26]*"* which I share. But is it that simple?

Determinism is a conception that, since some data are known, the facts that will follow will be precisely predictable. We see many areas of science confirming this reality. But it only takes an epsilon to vary the result over the course of the earth's time and the number of living things. This is where our free will comes in. We can at our level vary the epsilon which can itself contribute to vary the result with the space-time leverage effect. The butterfly effect, you might say? I prefer the leverage effect which better describes the logical consequence on space-time with the multiplication linked to reproduction. We are not independent, but we are autonomous.

We live in a world where the future is constantly changing because our present actions impact it. So, the future would already be written if we did not use our free will all the time. Our goal is to transform our potential futures from our intentions into alternative futures. Let us not forget that our direction is imposed on us but not the way to get there.

In the end, wouldn't it be the road taken that would be more important than the direction taken? By opting for one path rather than another, it is our collective future that evolves. The Russian writer Leo Tolstoy wrote *"The only meaning of life is to serve humanity"*. This corresponds to the seventh spiritual law of successful *"Dharma*[27]*"* which states that everyone has a unique gift to put at the service of others. It is now time to have the

---

[26] Le hasard, Revue du mois 3, 1907. Quote also attributed to Alfred Capus, Les pensées

[27] At the origin of Indian spiritualities and religions.

lucidity to serve the Universe, to serve this cosmic consciousness by developing and optimizing our resonance.

I therefore propose the following definition of destiny: *Pre-established determination of a direction to be taken during earthly life to optimize the development of cosmic consciousness.*

Level of soul expression and soul/consciousness autonomy

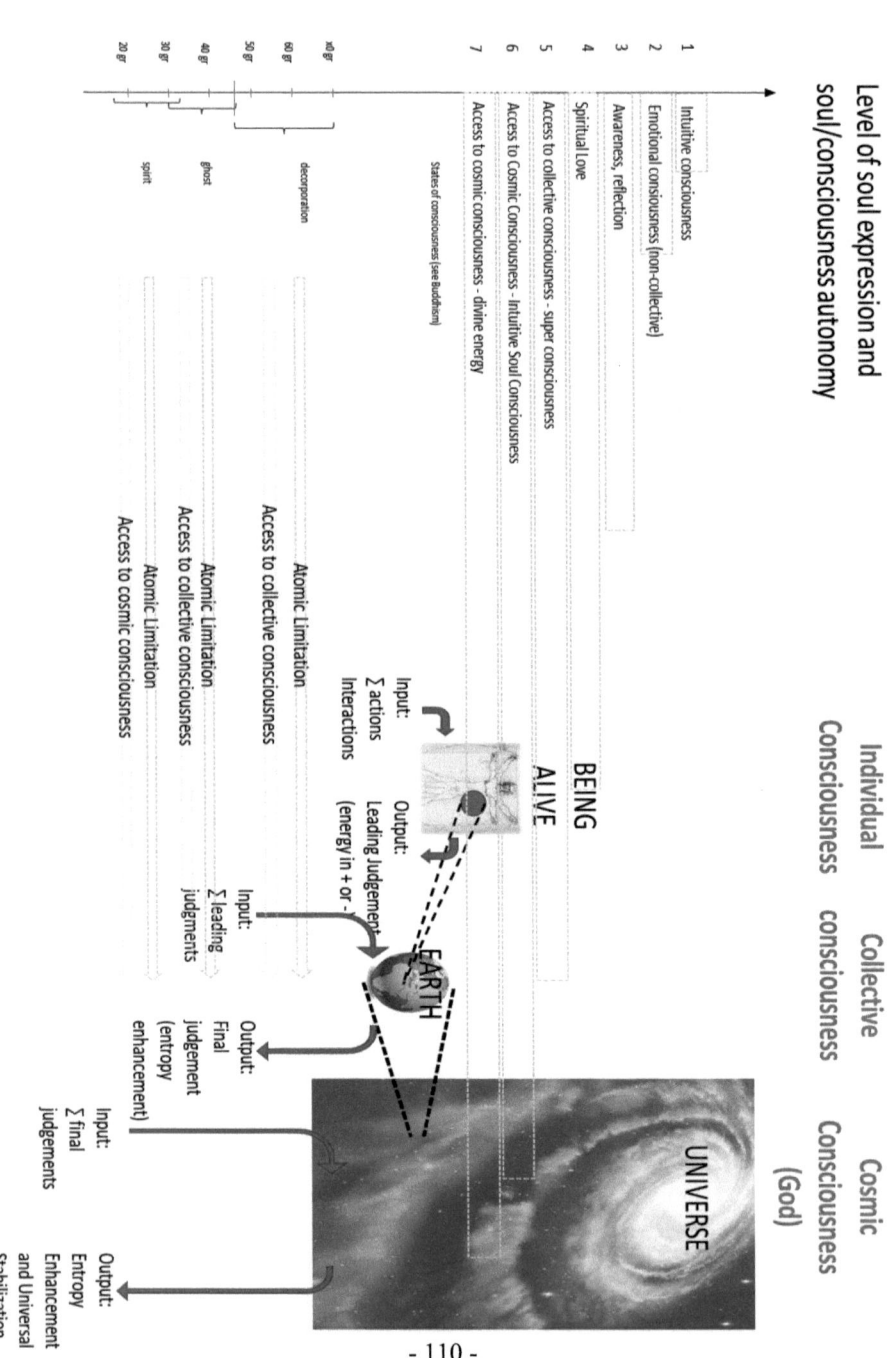

Individual Consciousness   Collective consciousness   Cosmic Consciousness (God)

1 Intuitive consciousness
2 Emotional consciousness (non-collective)
3 Awareness, reflection
4 Spiritual Love
5 Access to collective consciousness - super consciousness
6 Access to Cosmic Consciousness - Intuitive Soul Consciousness
7 Access to cosmic consciousness - divine energy

20 gr
30 gr
40 gr
50 gr
60 gr
×0 gr

spirit
ghost
decorporation

States of consciousness [see Buddhism]

Atomic Limitation
Access to collective consciousness
Atomic Limitation
Access to collective consciousness
Atomic Limitation
Access to cosmic consciousness

BEING ALIVE

Input:
Σ actions
Interactions

Output:
Leading Judgement
(energy in + or -)

EARTH

Input:
Σ leading
judgments

Output:
Final
judgement
(entropy
enhancement)

UNIVERSE

Input:
Σ final
judgements

Output:
Entropy
Enhancement
and Universal
Stabilization

Universe, Energy and Earth

I *believe*

I believe in a single, global Universe that we are building,
I believe in an energetic sap that unites us forever,
I believe in a mother planet that gives us free will,

I believe in Life as a whole,
I believe in our indispensable part in this Life,
I believe in a punctual life whenever we decide to.

I believe in an earthly life that is the source of all individual glory,
I believe in a historical dependency between spirits and their home planet,
I believe in a material world that supports the evolution of our mind.

I believe in a capital and universal role that we play in our earthly lives: our Destiny.

The Sleep Of A Life Time

Text by Diana McCormack (Cambridge, United Kingdom)

When your love ones close their eyes and fall into a deep sleep!
Why do we weep and mourn? Do you not realise they had to go
Home! They don't want to be awaken by all the screams and
Shouts! They just want to be at peace and enjoy their journey
Home!

The journey home might be far away, or it might be right next
Door, some say it's in another realm! The truth is we'll just
Never know until such time, only God knows when it will be.
It could yours or it could mine!

People will come and pay their respect, some you have not seen in a
while. Oh look! Fast asleep, they look so peaceful. Yes! Yes, they
are in a better place! May God bless them! And yet, you still cannot
come to terms with fact that they have just gone!

Remember! They have not gone forever and ever, they've just gone
ahead to see past love ones and old friends, and perhaps meet new
ones! But the day will come, when you'll laugh and hug again, but it
will just be in another land. They will be waiting at the pearly gate!

They will say welcome my love! Welcome my friend!

Acknowledgements:

My first thought goes to my reading committee, made up of friends who are interested in fundamental issues: Constance D. (Art Therapist), Danièle B. (Doctor of Medicine), Françoise V. (Retired teacher), Corinne D. (Educator), Roland G. (Computer architect), Alain S. (Retired security expert), Christian N. (Professor of physics), Philippe G. (retired). (Contractor), Teddy R. (Audit leader & Speaker), Diana MC. (Nurse and first reader), my mother (Retired palaeontologist) and my late father (Archaeologist).

Without forgetting Jean-Michel Ballester (Retired researcher teaching microbiology, Founder of Germe SA) who served as my guide for many years as well as Nadine Ottelard (Professor of Letters) who guided me in the world of publishing.

Thank you to all readers for sharing your time with me as you read this book.

If you wish to get in touch with me:
Mail : gillesbonifaydestinee@gmail.com
Facebook – La destinée terrestre
Facebook : https://www.facebook.com/profile.php?id=642093660